THE 10 BEST DECISIONS a LEADER CAN MAKE

THE 10 BEST DECISIONS *a* LEADER CAN MAKE

BILL FARREL

HARVEST HOUSE PUBLISHERS
EUGENE, OREGON

Cover design by Left Coast Design, Portland, Oregon

Cover photo © Shutterstock / pixelfabrik

The author is represented by the literary agency of Alive Communications, Inc., 7680 Goddard Street, Suite 200, Colorado Springs, CO 80920. www.alivecommunications.com.

THE 10 BEST DECISIONS A LEADER CAN MAKE
Copyright © 2013 by Bill Farrel
Published by Harvest House Publishers
Eugene, Oregon 97402
www.harvesthousepublishers.com

Library of Congress Cataloging-in-Publication Data
Farrel, Bill, 1959-
   The 10 best decisions a leader can make / Bill Farrel.
     pages cm
ISBN 978-0-7369-4540-0 (pbk.)
ISBN 978-0-7369-4541-7 (eBook)
1. Leadership—Religious aspects—Christianity. I. Title. II. Title: Ten best decisions a leader can make.
BV4597.53.L43F37 2013
253--dc23
                        2012041087

Printed in the United States of America

13 14 15 16 17 18 19 20 21 22 / BP-JH / 10 9 8 7 6 5 4 3 2 1

*This book is dedicated to Rick Verkerk and the faithful men
who oversee the ministry of Promise Keepers, Canada.*

*It has been an awesome privilege working with you to see
men's lives transformed. Your contagious leadership and
dedication to the principles that make a real difference in
men's lives has obviously been honored by our Savior.*

CONTENTS

This book has grown out of a desire that has been developing in my heart since I was in high school. I was the starting quarterback and the point guard on the basketball team, and I was often asked to run for student body offices. Within two months of beginning a personal relationship with Jesus at the age of sixteen, I was leading a Bible study with my brother. I was drawn to leadership, but I didn't know how to be a leader.

A series of faithful people, however, have helped me learn how to lead and then how to get the leadership principles on paper in a simple enough form for others to apply. My brother Jim was the first catalyst. Jim, you will never know how much confidence I gained when you told me in high school that it was exciting to play when I was the quarterback. You will also probably never fully appreciate the way leading a Bible study with you set the course for the rest of my life in ministry.

Meeting Pam at a college ministry conference was a better leadership move than I could ever have realized. Pam, you are one of the most effective and relentless leaders I have ever met. Your constant example of investing in others and leading the charge to help people grow is a constant source of inspiration to me.

Jack Peacock and the leadership group at Calvary Bible Church in Bakersfield, California, saw potential in me early on. Thank you men for investing in a young, idealistic pastor who made his share of mistakes as he figured out what it meant to lead with accountability.

I am forever indebted to the investment Jim Conway made in my life. Jim, I am still not sure what you saw in me that made you willing to spend time every week for four years investing in my growth, but I am extremely grateful. I learned how to apply skills, attitudes, and decision-making techniques I had read about from you. I can't imagine what my life would have been like without your input.

I want to thank Bob Hawkins and the entire staff at Harvest House Publishers. Bob, I love laughing with you as we dream about how to make a real difference in our world. Your staff is a refreshing collection of dedicated, mature professionals who have not lost the idealism that comes with faith in a big God.

Special thanks need to be extended to Rod Morris, who did an expert job editing the manuscript. Rod, thank you for clarifying my words, eliminating stories that were interesting but not relevant, and maintaining the integrity of the message. This book will help many more people because of your input. You have also won me over to being a Kansas State fan. One day we will watch them play for a national championship.

Finally, I want to say thank you to my Savior, Jesus Christ. You found me when I was sixteen in the padded seat of a movie theater and have taken me on a thrill ride ever since. It is humbly exhilarating to be in this remarkably unequal partnership.

Leadership Is You

I was talking with a young man recently who reminded me of the importance of leadership. He played football at the same school as one of my sons. I asked him how he decided on this particular school.

"When I first visited the school it was all about football, but then the coaches' lives got my attention. I was really impressed with the way they treated their wives and talked about their kids. I wanted to know if these men were for real.

"It still amazes me that the defensive coordinator invites us over to his house on Sundays to spend time with him and his family. He has a good marriage and a great relationship with his kids. He lives in a nice house. He has a good life, and I have seen in him what I want in my life."

It was one more example of the reason God calls us to lead. This young man came from a broken home. He respects his hardworking mom and has a loyal connection with his sister, but his dad is not in the picture. He wants to have a solid career, satisfying marriage, and successful family, but he didn't have a consistent male role model to pattern his life after. It is for people like him that the Bible challenges us to "set an example for the believers in speech, in conduct, in love, in faith and in purity" (1 Timothy 4:12). He found inspiration and confidence in the leaders who helped along his journey.

My List

We can all describe the journey of our lives by the leaders who have impacted us.

In third grade, Mrs. Svoboda taught me that math could be fun. She was energetic about math concepts and instituted a number of competitive games to help those of us with natural aptitude excel in our development. It was the first time in my life that learning captured the same sense of adventure as athletic competition. Her influence lingered all the way to college when I decided math would be a viable and enjoyable degree for me to pursue.

In fifth grade, I was assigned to Mr. Foladare's class. His body was mildly deformed from a childhood malady, but it never stopped him from doing what was on his heart. He taught with focus and enthusiasm that made me want to learn. He pitched for both teams during softball at recess. Even though he was only five foot six, he coached an elite club basketball team that consistently played in tournament championships. He was tough-minded, energetic, and determined that obstacles would not hold him back. He loved literature, which he read to us with gestures, animated voices, and enthusiasm. Through his influence, I began to think that books were more than just words on paper, and that eventually planted in me a desire for writing.

I entered my freshman year in high school with anticipation and hesitation. Coach Pitts started basketball practice that year with the statement, "You are going to be the toughest, hardest working team in our league. You may end up liking me or hating me by the end of the season, but you will be the most determined basketball players around." I wasn't even sure at the time why it got my attention. I do know, however, that my time with Coach Pitts better prepared me for the realities of life. When things don't work out the way I had hoped, I can hear his voice, "You can give just a little more." When I am exhausted by the responsibilities of life, I can hear his voice, "You are strong. You can do this." When the aches and pains of aging tempt me to give in, I can hear his voice, "Pain doesn't stop those who want to do their best."

Coach Howell was a high-school football coach in the mold of Paul "Bear" Bryant. He wasn't the most personable man I have ever met, but he knew how to win. He taught me that success is not just about talent. It's about maintaining discipline in the midst of adversity. It's about adjusting to challenges with a clear view of your goal and cultivating a mindset of believing you will succeed despite the forces trying to keep you from it.

Pastor Jack Peacock taught me the power of building authentic networks. He had an uncanny ability to connect with rugged men. Policemen had natural respect for him. Firemen called him a friend. Hunters and business owners alike were comfortable around him. He wasn't the most talented organizer and attending leadership conferences raised his stress level. He could, however, relate to real men in the midst of their real lives. He was also one of the most talented preachers when it came to altar calls. Every message he delivered ended with a call to commitment that motivated hundreds of people every year to trust in Christ as their Savior.

Bob Bell was a corporate leader I watched from a distance. He was extremely busy with his career and family so he didn't have much time to give, but the way he handled his life and business was attractive to me. An associate of his told me one day, "Bob was in charge of investigating safety reports in our company. He was always tough, but he was always fair. We always knew that when Bob reached a conclusion, it was going to be well-researched and fair to everyone involved." Observing Bob gave me confidence that hard decisions could be reached without destroying relationships.

Jim Conway convinced me that having a full-fledged ministry and raising a healthy family could be done at the same time. He was a professor in seminary, author, conference speaker, and devoted family man. He had an excellent relationship with his wife. His daughters spoke about him with high regard. Despite a difficult childhood, he was positive, energetic, and ambitious. While most people were telling me I should slow down, he was telling me I could live at an aggressive pace as long as I did it with intention and skill.

I could go on telling the history of my life with stories of how it has been shaped by teachers, ministry leaders, coaches, business professionals, and skilled family leaders. Given the opportunity, I believe you could do the same. You have developed your vocabulary through interaction with the leaders you respect. You have clarified your desires with input from those who have influenced you. You have shaped your thinking by testing it against the opinions and reactions of those you admire. You have discovered your areas of effectiveness by emulating those who have made a difference in you.

Before you go any further, make a list of the leaders who have helped shape your attitudes, decisions, and convictions.

The Promise

I suspect that you also are on someone's list. You said something at the right time, did something at a strategic moment, or were involved during an important phase of someone's development. You will be quoted for the rest of their lives. You will be remembered for your influence, your example, and your character. People will ask themselves, "What would [insert your name] do or say in this situation?" As leaders, we want to be confident enough to say, "Follow my example, as I follow the example of Christ" (1 Corinthians 11:1).

That's why I'm sharing my thoughts on leadership in this book. Since people are watching and making decisions based on what they see in us, it makes sense for us to be diligent in our personal development. As you work through this material, you will be challenged to grow in a number of areas, including:

Personal Character

The biblical view of leadership is that your influence is an extension of who you are, not just what you do. Jesus told his followers, "I am the vine; you are the branches. If you remain in me and I in you, you will bear much fruit; apart from me you can do nothing" (John 15:5). He saw influence as fruit we develop in our lives through a healthy connection with him. In another context, he said, "By their fruit you will recognize them...every good tree bears good fruit, but a bad tree bears bad fruit" (Matthew 7:16-17). Our leadership influence is the evidence of who we have become.

Paul picked up the same theme in his list of qualifications for church leaders: "[An elder] must be hospitable, one who loves what is good, who is self-controlled, upright, holy and disciplined. He must hold firmly to the trustworthy message as it has been taught, so that he can encourage others by sound doctrine and refute those who oppose it" (Titus 1:8-9). For Paul, spiritual leadership was not just an activity. It was a commitment to live out the message we represent. In 1 Timothy 3:5, he asked the probing question, "If anyone does not know how to manage his own family, how can he take care of God's church?"

Those of us who want to lead in a way that honors God and fulfills his purpose must accept that our leadership is an extension of our character. As Howard Hendricks says, "We cannot pass on what we do not possess."

Problem Solving

If people were fully functioning and the world were cooperative, leaders would not be necessary. You will face problems and you will need to overcome challenges regularly. In fact, the people who follow your leadership will assume you are skilled at guiding them to effective solutions. If we rush through our diagnoses and act on careless conclusions, we will only confuse those we are trying to lead.

> For more than 20 years Professor Edwin R. Keedy of the University of Pennsylvania Law School used to start his first class by putting two figures on the blackboard 4 2. Then he would ask, "What's the solution?"
>
> One student would call out, "Six."
>
> Another would say "Two."
>
> Then several would shout out "Eight!"
>
> But the teacher would shake his head in the negative. Then Keedy would point out their collective error. "All of you failed to ask the key question: What is the problem? Gentlemen, unless you know what the problem is, you cannot possibly find the answer."

This teacher knew that in law as in everyday life, too much time is spent trying to solve the wrong problem—like polishing brass on a sinking ship.[1]

If, on the other hand, we learn to assess our environment skillfully and train ourselves to uncover creative solutions, we will help others find new paths to success. Gregory E. Covey, a squad leader during a Marine training program, describes how trying something different led to success for his team.

Our mission was to take over a small village being held by the enemy (several well-trained Drill Instructors) with the ultimate goal of taking a hill beyond the adjacent woods.

Everyone before us had failed. My squad did accomplish the first successful mission of the day—and it was due to the fact that I altered the plan. I did not follow the norm that all the squads before had. I understood that everyone before had failed—why not try something different?

So we did. We approached the village from an entirely different direction surprising the Drill Instructors. We did the same for the hill we were to take. In that case we circled around the hill and came up from the back. We were rewarded by the Commanding Officer for being innovative and stepping out of the box.[2]

Practical Skills

Leadership involves motivating, organizing, honing, and coordinating the efforts of a variety of people for a common purpose. There are egos to manage, disagreements to mediate, agendas to steer, and talents to sync together. If you possess skills that are equal to the challenge, your journey can be rewarding. Highly effective leaders understand that today's success is based on yesterday's preparation. In training Timothy for his leadership role, Paul challenged him, "Be diligent in these matters; give yourself wholly to them, so that everyone may see your progress. Watch your life and doctrine closely. Persevere in them, because if you do, you will save both yourself and your hearers" (1 Timothy 4:15-16). Abraham Lincoln said it this way, "Give me six hours to chop down a tree and I will spend the first four sharpening the axe."[3]

Martin Luther King Jr. demonstrated the power of skilled nonviolence in his leadership of the civil rights movement. Jesus challenged his followers, "If someone slaps you on one cheek, turn to them the other also. If someone takes your coat, do not withhold your shirt from them" (Luke 6:29). Gandhi incorporated this principle into a system of resistance based on nonviolence and the absence of hatred, which Dr. King described as "the only morally and practically sound method open to oppressed people in their struggle for freedom."[4] As he skillfully applied the techniques, the movement realized dramatic strides forward, including the Montgomery bus riot involving Rosa Parks and the Washington march where he delivered his epic "I Have a Dream" speech.

If you lack sound leadership skills, however, your efforts become confusing and ineffective. Lincoln also stated, "It is better to remain silent and be thought a fool than to open one's mouth and remove all doubt."[5] Consider the frustration that resulted from everyone involved in the following story:

> A man in a hot air balloon was lost. He saw a man on the ground and reduced height to speak to him.
>
> "Excuse me, can you tell me where I am?"
>
> "You're in a hot air balloon hovering thirty feet above this field."
>
> "You must work in Information Technology," said the balloonist.
>
> "I do," said the man. "How did you know?"
>
> "Well," said the balloonist, "everything you told me is technically correct, but it's no use to anyone."
>
> "You must be in business," said the man.
>
> "I am," said the balloonist. "How did you know?"

"Well, you don't know where you are, you don't know
where you're going, but you expect me to be able to help.
You're in the same position you were before we met, but
now it's my fault." [6]

Talent Needs Direction

A quick look around will reveal a need for leadership at every turn.
Sometimes it's because people have talents that are powerful and persistent. They have as much potential for getting out of control and causing problems as they do for improving life. I looked around my world
recently and encountered the following talented people:

- One young man recently discovered he has a lot of passion
  and insight for business. With experience he has discovered that the steps to move his company forward are surprisingly clear to him. As a result, he grows impatient with
  other people in his company who question his directions
  and slow down the process. I was taken aback when he
  said, "If I don't learn how to be more patient with people, I
  think I'm going to lose my best opportunities."

- A missionary friend of mine was visiting in town and gave
  an update to different groups supporting his ministry. In
  his six years in Colombia, two thousand people have made
  professions of faith in Christ. It turns out that many in
  his congregation are gifted evangelists, but a conflict is
  brewing over what method is best for presenting the message. He was looking for advice on how to manage these
  strong opinions so conflict didn't interrupt the real work of
  evangelism.

- A young mom with a compassionate heart is raising a son
  with a compassionate heart. We discussed ways to help
  her son build discernment about how to truly help people.
  They both easily see the needs around them, but then they

get overwhelmed trying to figure out what, if anything, they should do about them.

- A friend of mine has a passion for good food, and he spent hours preparing tri-tip and cooking it to perfection. He asked if we could have our Bible study at his house so he could share his gift with us. We were excited about the offer, but frustration grew when my friend's enthusiasm over food threatened to eliminate time for the actual study. It took sensitive mediation to curb his enthusiasm and help the other members of the group adjust to encourage his efforts.

When talented people operate alone, no organization is needed. When you combine talents to accomplish a bigger goal, organization becomes the vital link to success. Everyone involved will feel their approach is best, so someone must coordinate the strengths into a cohesive system.

Deficiencies Need Training

At other times, leadership is needed because of the deficiencies in people's lives. "We all, like sheep, have gone astray, each of us has turned to our own way" (Isaiah 53:6). In an eternal sense, it took the death of Jesus to rectify the situation. In regards to human cooperation, it takes skilled leadership to accomplish goals when everyone involved is flawed.

Recently I met a farrier (someone who shoes horses), and I suspected he had some good stories to tell. I was not disappointed as he shared the following account about overcoming difficulties in others. Though the "other" in this case was not human, his story illustrates how effective leadership can accomplish goals in spite of the deficiencies of those being led.

"I was asked to shoe a particularly stubborn mule. When I first approached the animal, he would take off running just far enough to express his defiance. I tried all the usual tricks to create a relationship between me and the mule without success, so I knew I was going to have to outsmart this animal somehow.

"The most acute sense for mules is smell, so after I managed to rope him, I got a sweaty shirt from the laundry, put it over his head, and pulled his ears out of the armholes. I wanted him to be aware of me as I prepared him for the next lesson. I proceeded to attach one end of a fifty-foot rope to each of his front legs and tied the other end around an oak tree. Once I was confident the ropes were secure, I took the T-shirt off his head and untied the rope around his neck.

"The mule looked at me, and then defiantly took off running. About the time slack came out of the ropes attached to his legs, I yelled, 'Whoa!' The mule's legs came out from underneath him and he collapsed to the ground. He picked himself back up, snorted, and looked at me as if to say, 'How did you do that?'

"He still wasn't ready to give in, however, so he took off running in the opposite direction. Again, just as the slack came out of the ropes, I yelled, 'Whoa!' Again, the animal's front legs failed him and he crumpled to the ground. This time as he stood he looked at me with respect. He wasn't sure how I was able to do what I did, but he figured he better cooperate."

We laughed together and then I asked, "What would you do with a mule who absolutely refused to cooperate? Would you ever choose to not shoe him?"

He simply said, "You can't do that. Sometimes it seems impossible, but it has to be done anyway. You just stay at it until you figure out how to do the impossible."

His statement reminded me of Ecclesiastes 8:5-6:

> Whoever obeys his command will come to no harm,
> and the wise heart will know the proper time and procedure.
> For there is a proper time and procedure for every matter,
> though a person may be weighed down by misery.

Every Leader Counts

Everything God does on earth, he does with the help of leaders. Every great movement in history has been headed up by a leader. Even the most personal element of society (the family) is built around the leadership of a dad and mom. Every local expression of God's love and truth is guided by church leaders. Every business, large or small, rises and falls on the choices and skill of its leaders. Leaders are everywhere, and the need for them cannot be overestimated. Half the books in the Bible contain the word *leader,* and everyone in the church is called to "remember your leaders, who spoke the word of God to you. Consider the outcome of their way of life and imitate their faith" (Hebrews 13:7).

Welcome to the challenge and privilege of leadership. May you find new strength as you work through the principles in this book and grow in your ability to lead others.

CHAPTER 1

Decide to Be a Leader

You were born to be a leader. No matter who you are, no matter what family you were born into, no matter where in the birth order you find yourself, and regardless of the talents you either were or were not born with, you are a leader. The scope of your influence may be large or small, but you are a leader. You may influence only a handful of people in your lifetime or you may give direction to large organizations. Either way, you are a leader. You are a leader among your friends in some way. If you are married, you are a leader. If you are a parent, you are a leader.

Every arena of life needs leaders. Every collection of people brings together a diversity of interests, attitudes, and agendas. Without leadership, the imperfections in the hearts of these otherwise mutually invested individuals creates havoc, hurt feelings, and disharmony. God provided you as a leader, whether we call you father, mother, coach, director, manager, CEO, or mentor, to harness the potential and minimize the hurt when these talented individuals synthesize their efforts.

Check Out Your Childhood

That you are a leader is not an accident. God has been building your place of influence ever since you were born. To help determine your place of influence and the scope of your leadership, look back at the markers on your journey that point to what God has been doing in your life. As you read through the Bible, you will encounter many influential people with varied paths to their purpose.

Jacob, who was to become the patriarch of the twelve tribes of Israel, appears to have naturally been a manipulator. "He grasped his brother's heel" while in the womb (Hosea 12:3), he stole his brother's birthright (Genesis 25:29-34), and he had to wrestle with God in order to soften his heart (Genesis 32:22-32). Before Jeremiah was born, he was appointed to be "a prophet to the nations" (Jeremiah 1:5). This sounds noble and exciting except that his ministry was difficult. In his own words he said, "Why did I ever come out of the womb to see trouble and sorrow and to end my days in shame?" (Jeremiah 20:18). Perez had the misfortune of being born to scandalous parents, Judah and Tamar, only to have his genealogy lead to the birth of King David (Genesis 38:27-30; Ruth 4:18-22). John the Baptist was "filled with the Holy Spirit even before he [was] born" (Luke 1:15). An anonymous man was born physically lame and lived that way for decades before he met Peter and John, who healed him resulting in a great outburst of praise and amazement (Acts 3:1-10). Timothy grew up in a home that was spiritually focused so he was encouraged to "continue in what you have learned and have become convinced of, because you know those from whom you learned it, and how from infancy you have known the Holy Scriptures, which are able to make you wise for salvation through faith in Christ Jesus" (2 Timothy 3:14-15).

The circumstances are different but the principle is the same. God has been busy preparing us for our place of influence throughout our lives.

As I look back on my life, leadership was part of my journey before I was even aware of it. On the playground I was often asked to be a team captain who had responsibility for choosing up teams. In the classroom I was often asked to head up a project team, simple as the projects were. I didn't recognize it as leadership. I was just glad to be part of things.

In sixth grade, I was asked to be the master of ceremonies for the school Christmas program. I would introduce the program, manage transitions, and make strategic announcements. As part of the program, I joined the school choir. I would come out from the choir for my emcee responsibilities and then rejoin the singers. As practice began, it was obvious there was a problem. I first saw it in the face of the director. He had this twisted, sour look on his face. He could tell the choir was off-key, but he couldn't figure out why. It turned out it was me. I was singing off-key with enthusiasm. I was loud enough that I was pulling those near me off-key, and the wave spread from there.

I am still not sure why, but he decided to leave me in the choir. He did ask me to mouth the words without actually singing, however. Right on schedule, I came out of the choir for each transition and made my announcements from the podium. No one in the audience ever knew that I was a lip-syncing emcee. I have to conclude that the choir director left me in the choir because it was a good leadership move and it helped move the program forward.

I really had no business being in the choir. I couldn't tell what on-key even meant, and it wasn't for lack of training. My mom was a talented singer with a natural ear for music. My sister also had an ear for music, which motivated her to regularly sing in school choirs. My dad, my brother, and I were a different story. We all played the radio well and sang with enthusiasm, but none of us could tell the difference between a flat note and a flat pancake. Apparently, the music gene in my family is canceled out by the Y chromosome. [1]

It was, however, a significant moment in my leadership development. I wasn't wise enough at twelve years old to know what this meant, but I have reflected on that experience often and concluded that my place in leadership includes onstage activity and directing people. I also concluded my place does not include musical performance. It has helped me realize that when it comes to finding our places of influence, what we say no to is just as important as what we say yes to.

What Are Others Asking of You?

The next step in my discovery was a vague realization that people were asking me for advice. I considered myself to be just an average high school student with nothing more to offer than any of my peers. It seemed strange to me, then, that friends would ask with regularity if they could talk with me. Sometimes they would ask for help with school work. Sometimes they wanted my perspective on a relationship issue. At other times, they wanted to talk about their frustrations with their parents. I didn't understand why they were asking me, but it seemed important that I engage them.

Looking back, I understand now that this was the next step in my leadership journey. God was giving me previews of what was to come. I certainly didn't possess the wisdom, experience, or training to give authoritative advice or guide others with skill in their most important life decisions, but God had to start somewhere. As more people asked questions, I couldn't ignore the sense that this was part of what I was designed for.

When you look back at your childhood, what markers can you identify that help reveal God's design for your leadership?

Examine Your Experience

In lots of ways, we are all the same. In general terms, we were all born into a family, grew up with friends, and have some type of educational and career experience. In the details, however, we are all unique. We have had a series of experiences that create memories and force us to develop skills to adjust to our particular situation.

When it came time to choose a focus for my master's degree, I thought back to my own experience and the history of helping people that had accumulated. It made sense that I pursue a degree focused on helping others. I decided that all my elective classes during seminary would be in pastoral counseling. I wanted to learn all I could about people's personal growth, vital relationships, and obstacles to healthy living. Since people were inclined to ask me for help, I wanted to be as skilled as possible in leading them.

The Big Moment

But the experience that forever changed my journey happened when I was sixteen years old. I was independent and competitive and believed I could face any challenge with courage and skill. When my best friend asked me to spend the night with him so his dad could take us to a movie that was just out called *The Exorcist*, I honestly believed I could handle it. I expected to be mildly shocked by the special effects before I laughed off the movie's impact. It would be just another challenge to overcome. I had heard, however, that the movie was based on something true. That thought hovered around my mind as I watched the film. Somewhere along the way, the thought occurred to me, *I don't see any difference between me and the girl on the screen. I know Hollywood has overdone this, but if anything like that could happen to her, what would keep it from happening to me?*

I left with no answers.

My family didn't go to church and we didn't have any family friends so there was no one I could turn to for answers. We did, however, have a Bible in our house. I'm not sure if we had ever unzipped it, but it was in the house. I started reading the Bible each night before going to bed. I also started holding the Bible as I went to sleep because I had seen vampire movies and I was hoping the Word of God would provide protection in the same way a cross kept the creatures of the night away from potential victims. It was a miserable time because I was waking up frightened five or six times per night. I would read the Bible until I calmed down and then return to my fitful sleep.

After a month of this, I came across 1 John 4:4, "the one who is in you is greater than the one who is in the world." The light turned on in my soul. I sensed a need to do something, but I didn't know how to do what my soul was calling me to do. Fortunately, my brother had begun a personal relationship with Jesus a couple of months before.

I asked, "Jim, do you know how to get Jesus into your life, like 1 John 4:4 says?"

"Yes, I do," he said, "because a couple of months ago I asked him to live in me. It starts by admitting you need a Savior because you can't earn eternal life on your own. In addition, you want to acknowledge that he died on the cross to pay for your mistakes. Then you just sincerely ask him to live in you, forgive you for your sins, give you eternal life as a gift, and ask him to make you the person he knows you can be."

It was welcome news. It was just like starting a new friendship with a surprisingly big payoff. I was so concerned about finding peace from my personal turmoil that I failed to see the leadership lesson in what my brother did. He was the right leader in my life at the right time to help me take the next step. I had the need, but he had the plan that would meet that need. I was motivated to do something, but I didn't know what that something was. Because my brother had the conviction, interest, and understanding to lead me where I wanted to go, he became a very influential person in the early days of my spiritual journey.

Meeting Jesus was, without a doubt, the most exciting thing that ever happened in my life. Prior to that fateful night when I asked Jesus to live in me, I had relied on numbness to protect me from the irrational behavior in my home. Jesus wouldn't let me stay numb, however. An insatiable desire to learn suddenly arose inside me. An unexplainable drive to connect with others who also knew Jesus started to dominate my life. My brother and I weren't allowed to go to church because my mom was afraid of people, so church was not an option. We did manage to attend a few times and heard that we were supposed to study the Bible. We weren't exactly sure what that meant, but we knew we were supposed to do it.

Put Ideas into Action

Without being fully aware of it, we were being exposed to another characteristic of leaders: *leaders put ideas into action*. We recognized the importance of the call to study God's Word, so we gathered three other friends together to do our best at understanding the Bible. My brother started the evening by sharing what he had learned that week in his personal reading of Scripture. We then went around the room, taking turns sharing what we had learned in our own reading. I was the last to share, and I honestly didn't know what to do when we were done.

Someone in the group suggested we pray, so that's what we did. In our prayer time, we all agreed, "Jesus, this has been great tonight. Would you please double the size of this group?" Little did we know that God would answer that prayer the very next week when ten students showed up. We were amazed, so we again prayed for exactly the same thing. And the next week twenty high schoolers attended followed by forty the week after. At that point, we prayed, "Jesus, we don't know where we would put everyone if this keeps doubling, so you decide how big you want this to be. We will show up every week to share what we have learned. You decide who will join us."

The group grew to sixty, and our time together never got any more sophisticated than us going around the room sharing what God had taught us that week. It didn't seem like a big deal at the time because it was just the next thing to do. It was meeting such a big need in my life that I only casually recognized the leadership implications.

In the space below, describe an idea you have to make life better. What action can you take to see if this idea is something God will bless?

Prioritize the Needs You See

Looking back, I can see that God was orchestrating circumstances in our lives to prepare us for the leadership journey he had planned for us. Leaders see needs and set priorities to determine which are worthy of attention. Leaders set limits so they and their team can be as effective as possible. Leaders create environments in which other people can grow. Christian leaders are empowered by the Holy Spirit to make decisions. At times, they will perform well beyond their training and experience because of the active partnership they have with the Holy Spirit. My brother and I were too young and inexperienced to guide the kind of momentum our Bible study group generated, but we watched the working of God's Spirit turn this group into a vibrant, challenging, and encouraging collection of like-minded individuals.

My involvement in this on-campus Bible study during high school naturally led to involvement in an on-campus ministry in college where I learned my next step in this leadership journey. I had the opportunity to lead two young men to trust Jesus as their Savior. In response, I asked if they would like to form a discipleship group where I would teach them what I knew about having a relationship with Jesus. They both said yes, and it ended up being a milestone for me. I watched them grow as men. We talked about everything from how to read the Bible and pray, to how to tell your personal story so others could benefit from it, to relationships with young ladies, and how to overcome unhealthy patterns from the families we love.

This was the most fulfilling thing I had ever done. I was an architecture student and I enjoyed my studies a lot, but architecture didn't hold out for me the sense of destiny the discipleship activity generated in my heart. I grew up playing sports and loved competitive environments, but no athletic experience ever had the deep sense of personal reward that helping these guys grow had on me.

Passionate Pursuit

I didn't realize it at the time, but I was being introduced to the passion of leadership. Leading others is challenging, sometimes treacherous work. We challenge others to become more than they are today. We lead people in pursuits they could not pull off on their own. We develop teams of people who create synergy for significant accomplishments. In doing so, we often expose people's insecurities and inabilities. As a result, we will be confronted and challenged by those we are trying to help. When this happens, it is only the strength of your dedication to the vision that maintains your focus and commitment.

The ability of your passion for leadership to overcome the insecurities in others happens consistently at a corporate level. I was recently talking with my brother about a colleague at his work who is under-achieving. This coworker has parallel authority with my brother, but he lacks the skills to keep up with the demands of his position. He often comes to meetings and asks the other directors, "What should we do about this?" when "this" is in his area of responsibility. He is adept at making excuses for why his department was not able to deliver on time. His explanations sound plausible, but those closest to the situation know he is just stalling for time. Some of the projects my brother works on are rewarding and personally satisfying. For these, he has plenty of stamina to either work through or ignore the frustration with his colleague. On the more mundane projects, however, his colleague's lack of performance threatens to drain my brother of energy and makes him want to get away from his coworker and the project.

This is the nature of business as lofty goals intersect with an imperfect workforce. Businesses must be productive in order to maintain profitability, which creates the mandate that directs your efforts as a leader. As human resources are engaged to achieve the desired results, it soon becomes evident that every asset is flawed. Some people are proud and resistant to input. Others are hesitant to perform at their potential out of fear. Still others are hindered by personal insecurities that give rise to excuses and justifications for their poor performance. If you focus on these irritating deficiencies in people, you can't help but grow frustrated. If, however, you can remind yourself often of the passion that put you in this position, you can lead with vigor, determination and encouragement.

I remember when this came into focus for me. I committed to ministry as a profession because I love it. The reward of helping people grow is exhilarating. The responsibility of teaching God's Word feels like a privilege. As a result, I believe the church is the most important organization on earth and it is the steward of the most important message on earth. A passionate conviction to help churches grow strong guides my steps every day and I firmly believe churches ought to be the best run and best funded organizations on earth. The problem is that every piece is broken! They "all have sinned and fall short of the glory of the God" (Romans 3:23). The church will never be perfect. Significant members of the church will get in conflict over petty and ridiculous topics. Some people will get their feelings hurt over matters that don't really matter. Others will feel they have the right to be involved in ministries for which they are ill-prepared and overly opinionated.

When my focus is on the fallibility of the people, I can quickly get discouraged. When my focus is on the dignity of representing the Savior, however, it doesn't seem to matter as much. I want the people in my charge to seek excellence but I am not surprised by their shortcomings. I push for increased proficiency but I find the humor in the inconsistent development of those around me. My attitude is energized anytime someone begins a relationship with Christ, finds new hope in their marriage, or experiences a breakthrough in their personal growth because it reminds me of the passion that beats in my heart.

Parents as Leaders

The need for enduring passion to overcome the deficiencies in people is consistently on display at a family level also. Kids need parents to lead them since they begin life with no experience, no knowledge, and plenty of "foolishness in their hearts." The process of birth and infant bonding give parents a deep, personal connection to their offspring. When their kids make poor choices, throw tantrums, react emotionally immature, or struggle with areas of growth, connected parents have an endless well of dedication to draw from in handling these situations. These are, after all, our kids.

I know that I have no chance of being objective about my own children. I think they are brilliant, talented, full of potential, and incredibly insightful. At the same time, I have a vested interest in them not acting like idiots. I want them to make healthy decisions and have quality friends. I want them to be excellent husbands and fathers. As our sons were growing up, I was intense about addressing the issues in their lives as I became aware of them. I was intentional about leading them away from childish behavior and toward becoming mature and godly young men.

My oldest son, Brock, had a habit of being too hard on himself. When he was four years old, I heard an incessant banging on our garage door. I assumed he was throwing a ball against the door, and since it was getting annoying, I went out to tell him to stop. But what I saw stopped me in my tracks.

He was banging his head against the door and saying to himself, "Stupid, stupid, stupid…"

"What are you doing, Brock?" I said.

"I can't get the basketball to go through the hoop. I'm so stupid."

Correction and discipline were not what he needed at that point. What he needed was to learn grace. He needed to discover how to chill out, relax, give himself a break, and accept the imperfections of life. It has been a lifetime pursuit helping him learn contentment as he sets high goals.

The Daredevil

My middle son, Zachery, was the daredevil of the family. He started escaping from his crib as soon as he could walk. I was working in the yard one day when he was four years old. I heard him cry out, "Hey Dad, look at me."

I looked around but couldn't see any sign of him until he yelled, "No, Dad, up here!"

As I gazed upward, I noticed my son twenty-five feet up in a eucalyptus tree, swinging back and forth. I pictured the tree breaking, whipping my son across the yard and slamming him into the side of the house. But this was Zachery and he did this kind of thing all the time. After he figured out how to climb onto the roof of our church, he used to throw things up there so he could ask me if he could climb up and get it. "After all, Dad, we don't want God's house to be all messed up."

So when I saw him swinging in the tree, I shot up a quick prayer and continued on with my work. In typical fashion, he came up alongside me a few minutes later (unharmed, of course) and said, "Wow, that was fun!"

Along with his zest for life came an annoying lack of discernment. He just had a hard time figuring out the boundaries of life. He thought well into college that instructors determined their grades based on how much they liked you. I'm sure some teachers and professors operate this way, but it can't be all of them. He relied on anger as a way to relieve stress, resulting in a number of holes in the wall at the cheerleading gym he competed at during high school. When he left for college, we repainted his room only to find slice marks in the wall next to his bed.

I called to ask him, "Zach, what are all these slice marks in the wall from?"

"Oh, sorry, Dad. I was bored one night and I had a knife, so I guess I just started carving on the wall. I guess I should have told you."

The Sly One

My youngest son, Caleb, has always been the sly one. He doesn't announce his deficiencies or put his struggles on display. I honestly believe he thinks he is right most of the time and is prone to pride. He is subtle about it, however. When he was young, it manifested in stubbornness. He would constantly say, "Just one more thing," because he wanted the final word on everything.

"It's time to go to bed."

"Just one more thing."

"It's time to do your homework."

"Just one more thing."

"It's time to get dressed."

"Just one more thing."

"We aren't going to talk about this anymore."

"Just one more thing."

I loved his inquisitiveness and I was glad he wasn't passive, but "one more thing" became like a shrill car alarm that wouldn't stop.

In high school and college, he periodically would argue with his teachers or coaches. He did it with a respectful tone, but when he thinks he is right and others have missed the boat, he is determined to outlast their opinions. When he is right, it is exciting to watch his progress. When his perspective is off, however, it can be frustrating.

Whatever It Takes

The bottom line for me is that the challenges we faced with each of our sons were not deal breakers. I am attached to these young men in the deepest part of my soul. I believe in their abilities and I am convinced God created them with a purpose. I also believe they can figure out their calling and be successful at living it out. It doesn't matter to me what it costs to help them get there because I am totally invested in the process, and I am confident I was put on earth to help them discover their place of influence and live strong lives.

This is one of the reasons stepparents have a big adjustment. They care about the kids because they care about their new spouse, but they lack the intrinsic attachment one has with biological offspring. When the kids are easy and things are going well, it's fulfilling to be surrounded by your family. When the kids are difficult or one of them is in a self-inflicted crisis, it can be hard to find the motivation to do whatever it takes to help them get through the turmoil.

Dealing with Reality

Community organizations work best when leaders and coaches are passionate about the imperfect process of developing young men and women. I helped run the youth basketball league in our town for ten years. My kids were naturally athletic and I wanted them to have opportunities to learn about character building in competitive situations. I also grew up playing basketball so this was a comfortable setting for me. I loved coaching my kids, and I loved working with a dedicated group of volunteers who shared my love of the game and the opportunities to give kids a league to play in.

Some of the coaches shared this passion. They ran enthusiastic practices and competed skillfully on Saturdays. Other coaches did an adequate job because they believed in what we were doing, but they had no desire to excel in this venture.

Then there were the parents who had no business trying to coach, but they volunteered out of a misplaced sense of duty. They had kids in the league so they thought they should take their turn, but they either didn't like coaching or didn't know what they were doing.

One man in particular had a heart of gold, and outside the basketball gym he was a man of character. He had overcome physical obstacles in his life. He wore a leg brace and needed the help of a cane, but he was fully mobile and faced his setback with a great attitude. He worked in the people-helping profession and was quite skilled at helping others work through difficult situations and personal setbacks. Based on that, I figured he would be a great asset to our league.

But he didn't have any natural instincts for the game and had only minimal training. As a result, every aspect of the game was a big deal to him. He overworked practice and came to the first game with a crushing weight on his shoulders to perform well.

It didn't go well. The kids on the nine-to-ten-year-old team weren't very focused. His plans for them weren't being followed. The referees were not taking the game as seriously as he was. Eventually they made a call he didn't agree with and he erupted. All over the gym we heard his screaming, so a number of us headed to the court to see what was going on. When he raised his cane as if he were going to take a swing at the referee, we had to escort him out of the building and take over his team for the rest of that day.

The next day, he agreed he should not be the coach of the team. He felt overwhelmed and out of place. It was simply not in his heart to do this.

There is nothing wrong with admitting this, because we can lead only what we passionately believe in. I have been leading in ministry now for over thirty years because I am convinced that ministry is what God designed me for and it is vital in the lives of others. Two of my sons are coaching because they passionately believe in it. Helping young men and women find their potential and compete at their highest level is a conviction they hold in their hearts that gives them strength to work through bad attitudes, critical parents, and disappointing circumstances.

What people and pursuits are you passionate about?

God created you to inspire others to fulfill their God-given design and to finish the course of their lives. We never know what word or action is going to forever change the lives of those we interact with. Henning Mankell's perspective on life was forever clarified by two elderly, African men he encountered in Mozambique.

> I heard the two men talking about a third old man who had recently died. One of them said, "I was visiting him at his home. He started to tell me an amazing story about something that had happened to him when he was young. But it was a long story. Night came, and we decided that I should come back the next day to hear the rest. But when I arrived, he was dead."
>
> The man fell silent. I decided not to leave that bench until I heard how the other man would respond to what he'd heard. I had an instinctive feeling that it would prove to be important.
>
> Finally he, too, spoke.
>
> "That's not a good way to die—before you've told the end of your story." [2]

You are a leader and you have a story to finish. God is stirring your heart and preparing your life to accomplish his purpose in you.

> Take delight in the Lord,
>   and he will give you the desires of your heart.
> Commit your way to the Lord;
>   trust in him and he will do this:
> He will make your righteous reward shine like the dawn,
>   your vindication like the noonday sun.
>   (Psalm 37:4-6)

CHAPTER 2

Decide to Pursue Your Personal Vision

God has deposited a dream in the heart of every person. It is evident in the unique DNA that only you have. It is evident in the spiritual gifts God gave you when you met Jesus. It is evident in the unique combination of talents and abilities you possess. It is also evident in the internal drive we all have for something bigger than everyday life.

Ephesians 2:10 states, "For we are God's handiwork, created in Christ Jesus to do good works, which God prepared in advance for us to do." When God created you, he did so with a purpose in mind. At the point of salvation, the Holy Spirit indwelt you and began to energize that purpose so you could recognize the dream that has been placed in your soul. That purpose is designed to be understood, expressed, and lived out. This is why you have a stirring in your heart as a leader. There is something that, in your opinion, must be done while you are on earth. It makes you restless at times, driven at times, and deeply satisfied when you actually see your dream in action. An agonizing dissatisfaction also haunts you when your life is not actively involved in implementing the dream that burns within you.

Developing a *personal vision* is a way of identifying your dream in terms that give guidance to your goals and decisions. You identify the dream in your soul, express it in words, and direct it with goals and activities.

A *vision statement* is a simple summary of this vision that inspires you. You know you have discovered it when you read it and:

- It makes sense to you.
- Something stirs in your heart.
- It contains a big idea.
- Your energy level rises.
- You realize you have found what makes you tick.
- You feel compelled to do something about it before you die.
- It is simple enough to be easily remembered.

A personal vision is one of the primary characteristics that makes you a leader. Everyone on earth has equal value and everyone's contribution to life is important, but every team, every process, and every organization needs leaders. And God is the one who stirs up the heart of the leader with a vision that must be put into action.

When God Stirs Your Heart

There are numerous examples in the Bible of how God identifies leaders by stirring their hearts.

During the early days of Ezra, the nation of Israel was in a pathetic state. The walls of Jerusalem were piles of rubble and the temple was nonexistent. It was embarrassing to proclaim the God of Abraham, Isaac, and Jacob as the ruler of the universe and Creator of all life when his "earthly house" had been dismantled by mere men. People of faith understood that the exile of the nation that made it possible for human foes to take the temple apart was the result of God's own hand of discipline. His children had refused to repent, so he eventually put them in a time-out until their hearts changed. When it came time to rebuild,

> The LORD moved the heart of Cyrus king of Persia to make a proclamation throughout his realm and also to put it in writing:

"This is what Cyrus king of Persia says:

"'The LORD, the God of heaven, has given me all the king-
doms of the earth and he has appointed me to build a temple for him at Jerusalem in Judah. Any of his people among
you may go up to Jerusalem in Judah and build the temple
of the LORD, the God of Israel, the God who is in Jerusalem, and may their God be with them. And in any locality
where survivors may now be living, the people are to provide them with silver and gold, with goods and livestock,
and with freewill offerings for the temple of God in Jerusalem'" (Ezra 1:1-4).

When the vision is large, God stirs the hearts of other leaders also
to move the plan forward. Such was the case for rebuilding the temple. "Then the family heads of Judah and Benjamin, and the priests and
Levites—everyone whose heart God had moved—prepared to go up
and build the house of the LORD in Jerusalem" (Ezra 1:5). The vision
in this case was to build a temple for the God of Israel at Jerusalem. It
was a simple statement of the heart that was able to mobilize the entire
community to selfless action.

The rebuilding of the temple was a glorious achievement, but it created a problem. The completion of the temple project ushered in a new
habit of enthusiastic worship in the city of Jerusalem. This revived the
attention of those who did not want the Jewish people to prosper, and
they were vulnerable because the walls were not rebuilt. Anyone at any
time could march into the city unimpeded to do harm. The need gave
rise to a new vision in the heart of Nehemiah.

Hanani, one of my brothers, came from Judah with some
other men, and I questioned them about the Jewish rem-
nant that had survived the exile, and also about Jerusalem.

They said to me, "Those who survived the exile and are
back in the province are in great trouble and disgrace. The
wall of Jerusalem is broken down, and its gates have been
burned with fire."

> When I heard these things, I sat down and wept. For some
> days I mourned and fasted and prayed before the God of
> heaven (Nehemiah 1:2-4).

Nehemiah's vision, like Ezra's, was simple and compelling. We will rebuild the wall in the shortest amount of time possible.

Unlikely Heroes

Esther was an unlikely hero. Her greatest asset in life was her good looks, which opened the door for her to eventually become the queen of Persia, even though she was a Jew. People would have easily identified her as a model but no one would have spotted her as the rescuer of her people. The nation of Israel was on the verge of elimination because of a deceptive plot devised by Haman, the right-hand man of the king of Persia. The need for action in response to this plot first gripped Mordecai, Esther's cousin, who "tore his clothes, put on sackcloth and ashes, and went out into the city, wailing loudly and bitterly" (Esther 4:1). When Esther discovered from Mordecai the drastic threat to her people, a vision was born in her heart.

> Then Esther sent this reply to Mordecai: "Go, gather
> together all the Jews who are in Susa, and fast for me. Do
> not eat or drink for three days, night or day. I and my attendants will fast as you do. When this is done, I will go to the
> king, even though it is against the law. And if I perish, I perish" (Esther 4:15-16).

Esther's vision was ambitious, courageous, and potentially dangerous, but it was simple to state, "You fast and pray. I will talk to the king. Together, we will see if God delivers our people."

Some people have their heart stirred out of personal pain or disappointment. Hannah was one example. Although she had a great relationship with her husband, she was deeply disappointed by her inability to have children. She knew she ought to be content because her marriage was intact, she was healthy enough to work, and she understood that God loved her. But the desire for a child would not subside. Her vision wasn't birthed out of inspiration, success, or daydreaming.

> In her deep anguish Hannah prayed to the LORD, weeping bitterly. And she made a vow, saying, "LORD Almighty, if you will only look on your servant's misery and remember me, and not forget your servant but give her a son, then I will give him to the LORD for all the days of his life, and no razor will ever be used on his head" (1 Samuel 1:10-11).

The decision to give up your son to be raised in the temple, living as a selfless servant all the days of his life, is neither pleasant nor popular.

There are days, of course, when any of us would willingly hand off an impossibly difficult child to someone else to raise, like the father who reported the following story to me:

> I was in a department store with my four-year-old daughter. She was unruly, complaining loudly, and arguing about everything. After numerous failed attempts to calm her down and convince her to be cooperative, I finally picked her up and carried her out of the store. As we exited, she squirmed frantically in my arms and called out to the security guard, "Help me. This is not my dad!"

We are not, however, talking about taking a break from an irritating child. Hannah was offering to present her son, should God give her one, to be raised in the temple as a world-changing servant. It is a noble and honorable request, but it was also incredibly difficult. It's as if God knew the only way to convince Hannah to accept this particular purpose for her life was through the crucible of personal pain.

Again, the vision was stated simply, "I will give [my son] to the LORD for all the days of his life." It had implications that affected her entire life. It captured the passion of her heart. It gave her courage to face the challenges inherent in her decision. And yet it could be stated in a single sentence.

It's a Process

In various ways and by various means, leaders discover a vision that guides them, drives them, helps them make decisions, and compels them to stay at it until the dream has been fulfilled. Discovering your personal vision statement is a process. You may sit down once to work on it and find that it falls together for you, but that is not the norm. It is more common for your vision to clarify over time.

The first time I wrote my personal vision it was too long to hold my interest and too complicated to be remembered. It contained the seeds of what was important to me, but it was not user-friendly. Here is my first draft written during my thirties:

> I, Bill Farrel, am committed to teaching God's Word in a way that helps people put it into practice in their daily lives. I am committed to the important relationships in my life, which include my relationships with God, my wife, my kids, and my friends. I want to help people live better lives, and I want others to say their relationships worked better because of our association with each other.

For a couple of years, I lived with this statement and tried to make it work for me. I liked it, but it was difficult to remember, and I found myself rambling any time I tried to explain it to someone else. So I committed myself to modifying it. I made it a topic of my prayer life, asking God to give me the wisdom to make it simpler. I would spontaneously rewrite it every once in a while as a new rendition occurred to me.

Since your personal vision statement is a reflection of the dream that resides in your heart, it may rise to the surface at any time with renewed clarity and enthusiasm. I rewrote my statement on an airplane, in my office, in my garage, and at a local coffee shop. It took a few attempts, but I finally settled on this:

> *I, Bill Farrel, am committed to help as many people as possible grow in their most important relationships.*

This simple statement carries an abundance of implications for me. Among them are:

- It is personal to me, which is why I put my name on it.
- I am willing to pay a high price to accomplish this because it is a commitment.
- The core of my dream is helping others.
- The core of my dream involves relationships.
- The potential is limitless because it is focused on "as many people as possible."
- My dream is skill-based because I want people to grow in their relational abilities.
- My dream involves priorities because it is focused on the most important relationships.
- Multiple methods can be employed, which could include local church ministry, education, book writing, conference speaking, media appearances, small group curriculum, and many options that either don't yet exist or I have yet to discover.

Made to Mature

It's normal for your vision statement to evolve over time; consider two well-known companies whose statements have changed:

- In 1970, Honda's vision statement was, "We will destroy Yamaha." It has evolved into, "To Be a Company that Our Shareholders, Customers and Society Want."
- In the 1960s, Nike's vision statement was, "Crush Adidas." Currently it is, "To be the number one athletic company in the world."[1]

These are very large companies with complex, interconnected departments, but they are inspired by a simple, passionate statement of the purpose behind their existence. Similarly, our lives are a complex collection of commitments, decisions, and relationships. It's easy to get lost in simply doing the next thing in an attempt to keep up with responsibilities. This is admirable because it leads to a disciplined, reliable life, but it will lack passion, motivation, and voluntary dedication if it isn't guided by a personal vision.

You may be asking at this point, "Do I really need to write a vision statement?" The answer, of course, is no you don't *have* to write a vision statement. But you will find more clarity in your decisions and more confidence in your influence if you go through the process of committing your vision statement to paper.

Everyone Wants to Follow a Vision

The year was 2012. I was in Louisville during the Final Four basketball matchup between the University of Louisville and the University of Kentucky, which was being played in New Orleans. People all over Louisville were obsessed. The place where we ate lunch gave a free appetizer to anyone who wore apparel from their school of choice. Cars were decorated with red and blue flags. Family members argued with one another over which team was better.

Riots even broke out on the streets of Lexington, home of the University of Kentucky, when the Wildcats won the game.

> College antics in alcohol-fueled celebrations of UK's Final Four victory quickly escalated, as young people set couches and two cars ablaze and hurled beer cans into clusters of party-goers.
>
> Firefighters responded to about 50 nuisance fires, mostly couches set afire on purpose, according to Battalion Chief Ed Davis of the Lexington Fire Department. Ten people were injured, he said...
>
> Revelers climbed atop cars, flipped three vehicles on State Street to the cheers of others and attempted to flip others while fans chanted "Cats, Cats, Cats..."

Joey Frederick, who joined the revelry in Lexington, said Saturday's win warranted a party on campus. "We are the best team in America," he said. "I think houses should burn."[2]

Prior to the game, an altercation broke out at a dialysis clinic between a sixty-eight-year-old Kentucky fan and a seventy-one-year-old Louisville fan as the men argued about who would win. The fight likely wouldn't have surprised Kentucky coach John Calipari, who lovingly compares Wildcats fans to piranhas—yes, the flesh-eating fish.

The point of sharing all this is to illustrate that everyone wants to be attached to something big. They dress for their teams. They shout for their teams. They plan their schedules around their team's competitions.

God has placed a dream for significance in the heart of everyone he created. Hopefully we add discipline and common sense to our aspirations, but there is no quenching the desire to be significant. Having a personal vision for your life is simply putting into words the dream that stirs within you.

So, how do we as leaders go about discovering the dream that is intended to raise our motivation and focus our decisions? The process consists of a number of lingering questions that position our hearts and minds to discover the purpose we were created for. Your answers to these questions form an intersection of ideas at the point of your purpose. If you are interested in making your vision statement clearer, start by asking yourself the following.

What Do You Love in Life?

Proverbs 4:23 states, "Above all else, guard your heart, for everything you do flows from it." Your heart has a relentless way of expressing itself. If you love your work, you find ways of doing more of it. If you love relationships, you will find yourself drawn to conversations and experiences that connect you with people. If you love to build, you will commit to projects. If you love technology, you will find a place in your budget for the latest gadgets. The dream God placed in your heart will be reflected somehow in everything you do.

Where Do You See God Working in Your Life?

Proverbs 19:21 says, "Many are the plans in a person's heart, but it is the LORD's purpose that prevails." You will notice that some areas of your life work better than others. If God wants to teach others through you, people learn remarkably well when they are around you. If God organizes through you, other people are more efficient when they work in your systems. If God intends to encourage others through you, you will notice that others are happier and more confident after they spend time with you. You will see these kinds of results because "the LORD's purpose prevails" in these areas of your life.

What Are the Ideas You Cannot Get Away From?

David was a remarkable leader who led the nation of Israel on the most successful military campaign of its history. God's hand of favor was obviously on him as he won battle after battle. There was, however, a stirring in his heart to build a house for his God. It bothered him that his house was nicer than the place they went to worship God. He understood the reasons it was that way, but he couldn't escape the nagging thought that it just wasn't right. He announced to all the leaders in his kingdom,

> "Listen to me, my fellow Israelites, my people. I had it in
> my heart to build a house as a place of rest for the ark of the
> covenant of the LORD, for the footstool of our God, and I
> made plans to build it. But God said to me, 'You are not to
> build a house for my Name, because you are a warrior and
> have shed blood'" (1 Chronicles 28:1-3).

If David's vision to build a house for his God were just an idea, he would have grown frustrated when God told him he personally couldn't do it. It would have lost its luster and dropped out of his heart. But it was more than an idea, it was part of the dream God had placed in his heart. So David adjusted. Since he couldn't build the house, he drew up the plans and stockpiled the resources that were needed to construct it. He found great joy in giving to the project: "'But who am I, and who are my people, that we should be able to give as generously as this? Everything comes from you, and we have given you only what comes from your hand'" (1 Chronicles 29:14). He was thrilled to give his son Solomon "the plans for the portico of the temple, its buildings, its storerooms, its upper parts, its inner rooms and the place of atonement" (1 Chronicles 28:11). He was able to live out his vision even though he never actually saw the construction of the building.

What Would You Ask for If You Could Have Anything?

Solomon was given this opportunity to ask for anything, and his response has challenged everyone who has ever read the account. "God appeared to Solomon and said to him, 'Ask for whatever you want me to give you'" (2 Chronicles 1:7). Anything! He could ask for anything and God would give it to him. No restrictions, no qualifications, no conditions. Wow, what would you ask for?

Solomon searched his heart to see what was really there. He had no reason to ask for anything other than what he really wanted since God had removed all the barriers. Solomon's simple response to God's offer is the stuff a personal vision is made of. "Give me wisdom and knowledge, that I may lead this people, for who is able to govern this great people of yours?" (2 Chronicles 1:10). To put it in simplest terms, his vision was to be the wisest man on the face of the earth. (You probably know Solomon's history and are aware that though God granted his request, Solomon often did not follow the wisdom that was given to him.)

What Themes Repeat Themselves During Your Devotional Life?

Psalm 37:4 states, "Take delight in the LORD, and he will give you the desires of your heart." The dream God put in your heart rises to the surface whenever you spend personal time with him. He made you for this. He is excited about what you can do with it. He loves watching you in action! As a result, he reminds you of his dream for you anytime you give him an opportunity.

What Makes You Feel as Though Your Life Is Important?

Since we live in a broken world, some activities, such as taking out the trash and routine cleaning, can be dull and lifeless. They are neces-sary, but they are powerless to bring any sense of real fulfillment. If you give these common activities too much attention, they become distrac-tions or worse. Some activities, however, reflect your true purpose and carry the potential to bring a strong sense of fulfillment and impor-tance to your life. They may be intimidating at times because they are so powerful, but they are the pursuits you were created to be involved with. As a result, when you are engaged in them, you feel alive, valu-able, and energized. The apostle Paul put it this way:

> In a large house there are articles not only of gold and silver, but also of wood and clay; some are for special purposes and some for common use. Those who cleanse themselves from the latter will be instruments for special purposes, made holy, useful to the Master and prepared to do any good work (2 Timothy 2:20-21).

What Consistently Gets Interrupted in Your Plans?

Isaiah described the process in chapter 30. Verse 1 begins with the declaration,

> "Woe to the obstinate children,"
>   declares the LORD,
> "to those who carry out plans that are not mine,
>   forming an alliance, but not by my Spirit,
>   heaping sin upon sin."

God placed a dream inside you because it is part of his plan and is designed to be the best way for you to live. When you cooperate with the plan, God leads with simplicity and encouragement. Each of us, however, has the ability to come up with our own plans that may or may not be in line with God's plan. When our plans conflict with his, he faithfully interrupts them and frustrates their execution, because "the LORD longs to be gracious to you; therefore he will rise up to show you compassion…Whether you turn to the right or to the left, your ears will hear a voice behind you, saying, 'This is the way; walk in it'" (30:18,21).

What Activities in Your Life Cause Real, Measurable Growth?

One of Jeremiah's jobs was to remind the nation of Israel that their exile to Babylon was temporary and they would eventually return to their homeland. In his exhortation, we see the heart of God as it relates to his plan for the future of Israel: "For I know the plans I have for you," declares the LORD, "plans to prosper you and not to harm you, plans to give you hope and a future" (Jeremiah 29:11). Though Israel's situation looked hopeless, God was not finished with his people. He still had plans to prosper the nation and give her a future.

God likewise has a plan for each of us, the dream he has planted in our hearts. Jeremiah describes a number of characteristics of these dreams:

- They will prosper our lives.
- They will not harm us.
- They develop hope.
- They create a positive future.

In other words, they create real progress in our lives. We may not become as rich as we want or as secure as we can imagine, but we will see real, distinguishable growth in our life as we pursue his plan. This same priority is echoed in 2 Peter 3:18, where we are instructed to "grow in the grace and knowledge of our Lord and Savior Jesus Christ."

What Behaviors Would You Be Willing to Defend No Matter Who Questioned You?

Just as schools have tests, athletic teams put their skills on display in contests, and work projects have deadlines, so our lives were created with checkpoints to evaluate our progress. Some of these points are brought on by transitions in our lives which lead to times of honest evaluation before God. At these moments, we assess our abilities, evaluate our decisions, and clarify our convictions. These quizzes along the way help us determine the difference between our preferences and our convictions. We don't know how solid our belief in biblical truth is until we are criticized or persecuted for our faith. We don't know how dedicated we are to marriage until we face times of unhappiness and conflict. We don't know if we are committed to our career path until there are challenges to persistently overcome. We don't know if the way we treat people is an act or part of our personal ethics until we have to deal with difficult colleagues. The convictions that stand the test of time are expressions of your personal vision.

These evaluations along the way prepare us for the encounter we will experience at the end of our journey when we give an account of life to our Creator. God created each of us for a purpose, and he is working to help us live it out. The final exam reveals how well that purpose was fulfilled.

> "I the LORD search the heart
>   and examine the mind,
> to reward each person according to their conduct,
>   according to what their deeds deserve."
>   (Jeremiah 17:10)

He is going to sit down with each of us and lead us in a thorough, purposeful review of our decisions and personal development. We will have an opportunity to describe what we have done with what we were given. To be sure, some of what we will talk over with our Savior will be uncomfortable since we are all imperfect, but some of what will be covered will be exciting and rewarding to talk about. As you are able to identify the topics you look forward to discussing with him, you gain insight into the dream you were designed to live out.

What Goals Come to Mind Repeatedly as You Read God's Word?

James wrote to a group of believers who were living in intense times. They needed bottom-line instructions filled with simple illustrations so they could apply the principles efficiently. In James 1:22-25, he compares reading the Bible to looking in a mirror. Each time you "look" at God's Word, you can see the way God made you and the desires he has planted in your heart. For a brief moment, you make adjustments to your life and get refocused. "Whoever looks intently into the perfect law that gives freedom, and continues in it—not forgetting what they have heard, but doing it—they will be blessed in what they do" (1:25). Taking note of the ambitions that come to mind as you inter-act with the Bible will help you discover the dream God has planted in your soul.

Identifying Your Personal Vision

Step 1: Answer probing questions. Work through the questions listed above. Without rushing yourself, write a short paragraph in response to each question. Don't worry about whether you have the right answers. Just put your thoughts on paper.

Step 2: Take a break. Once you have brainstormed through the ques-tions, take a little time off to give your mind an opportunity to rest. Writing your thoughts out is like planting seeds, which need time to take root in your soul. As you give these thoughts time to germinate, they often get clearer.

Step 3: Look for recurring themes. The dream God placed in your heart demands to be expressed. Whenever you take time to think, the dream runs to the front of the line and volunteers to answer your ques-tions. As it matures, it may not be concise or simply stated, but it finds ways of showing up in your writing. The thoughts that captivate you will repeat themselves often enough to point you toward God's vision for your life.

Step 4: Use the recurring themes to write a vision statement. Don't worry about how long or short it is. Don't worry about the grammar of your sentences. Don't worry about whether it is the best statement you've ever written. Just get something on paper.

Step 5: Live with your statement for a while. Give it a few weeks to a few months. Print it and hang it up somewhere you will see it often. Put it on your computer and your phone so you can refer to it at any time.

Step 6: Review your vision statement by asking the following questions:

- Does this vision statement make sense to me?

- Does it stir my heart?

- Does it contain a big idea?

- Does it cause my energy level to rise?
- When I read it, do I realize I have found what makes me tick?
- Is it simple enough to be easily remembered?

Core Values

Your dream is the map to the best of who you are. As a result, it is energized and directed by the values you hold most dear. Making a list of your core values helps you test whether your vision statement is truly a reflection of your dream or just an exercise you went through. Also, your core values help you maintain your focus as you work out your dream in real life. Every action in your life has multiple ways in which it can be pursued. Consider the following scenarios:

You get a new position at work with oversight responsibility. You have the freedom to set your own hours. You can arrive at work before the rest of the work force to set an example. You can arrive at different times on different days as a way of checking on the work habits of those you are responsible for. You can use your freedom to set a schedule that works best for your family. Your decision will flow out of your core values.

You win the lottery or receive a sizeable family inheritance. You can spend quickly on everything you have always wanted. You can give to the charities of your choice. You can help out everyone in your circle of family and friends. You can invest every dollar and live off the interest. These options only scratch the surface of possible ways to use the money, but the ones you will consider emanate from your core values.

Your kids enter high school where they wrestle with important decisions about relationships, educational pursuits, moral choices, extracurricular involvements, and career paths. They may be athletes, musicians, student body officers, or nearly invisible members of their class. As they transition to adulthood, they may choose to be mechanics, secretaries, salespeople, business owners, factory workers. They may remain single or get married. They look to dependable adults around them for advice, and the opinions you offer up will be extensions of your core values.

How do you identify your core values? The process of identifying what truly drives you is a journey into listening to yourself. You hold convictions in your heart and you express those convictions in the sayings you repeat often, the decisions you make, and the way you spend money. If you are willing to look at the history of your life, you will become familiar with your core values, which ought to include, at minimum, statements that cover the following areas:

Work Ethic
- How hard do you like to work?
- How do you determine when you are finished with a task?

Excellence
- What does excellence mean to you?
- How important is it to you to do things with excellence?

Priorities
- How do you determine what is important to you?
- How do you determine what to do first?

Spiritual Dependency
- What role does God play in your everyday life?
- How involved do you want God to be in your decision making?

Quality Control
- How do you decide when something is "good enough"?
- How do you determine when something needs to be redone?

Moral/Ethical Considerations
- What do you consider to be morally acceptable?
- How do you think people ought to be treated?

Take a few minutes to write in the space below short answers to these questions, and then add any other statements you think might qualify as your core values. Then boil them down into the fewest number of statements you are comfortable with.

My Core Values

As I stated previously, my personal vision is to help as many people as possible grow in their most important relationships. In order to do this, I believe I need to stick to the following core values:

- I will test all my decisions to see if they are compatible with biblical truth. (Spiritual Dependency, Excellence)

- I will ask God for wisdom prior to making decisions. (Spiritual Dependency)

- I will do everything with excellence according to its priority in my life—A priorities get A effort, B priorities get B effort, and so on. (Excellence, Work Ethic, Priorities, Quality Control)

- I will treat everyone with equal respect since they were all created in the image of God. (Moral/Ethical Considerations)

- I will do what is right simply because it is the right thing to do. (Excellence, Quality Control, Moral/Ethical Considerations)

- I will regularly take appropriate risks. (Quality Control)

- I will seek to live out whatever I teach others. If I am not doing it, I will not export it. (Moral/Ethical Considerations, Quality Control)

- I will work as hard as current goals require. (Excellence, Work Ethic, Quality Control)

You will notice that each of these statements applies to various areas of life. This is because our lives are seamlessly integrated. We don't have moral convictions that are separate from our spiritual values that are separate from our work ethic. Our core values direct everything we do and say.

Once you get your core values written, live with them for a few weeks, and then ask yourself if you are truly living by them. This is helpful because all of us talk better than we live. It is exactly why we have a Savior and why he sent the Holy Spirit to be our helper. All of us have expressed our opinions, either in spoken words or in writing, only to find that they were just intellectual preferences that were not strong enough to withstand the demands of real life. We always live by our values, so each of these moments serves as an opportunity to either change our core value statements to match our behavior or set a plan for personal growth to help us mature into our values.

CHAPTER 3

Decide to Be Ready

One of my best friends is Captain Jack. He serves on our city's police force and often has interesting stories to share. One of my favorites involves a man who was arrested on suspicion of stealing a woman's purse. He was put in a lineup with four other men so the victim could try her hand at making a positive identification. The first man in line was told to take a step forward and say, "Give me your purse." Before he could respond, the suspect blurted out, "That's not what I said."

Many of Jack's stories are much more intense than this and contain an element of imminent human risk. As he was relating one of these stories to a group of mutual friends, somebody asked, "Don't you get afraid when you face certain situations on the street?"

He calmly replied, "I live by the motto, 'Be ready so you don't have to get ready.'"

On any given day, you will be asked questions, presented with problems, confronted with new opportunities to evaluate, and forced to adjust to new competition and new technologies. You don't want to begin preparing for these contingencies after they happen. You want to live in a state of readiness so you can focus your efforts and resources on positive steps of progress.

None of us, of course, can prepare for every contingency we will face. Most of us would view that as boring even if it were possible. It is in our best interests, however, to live with an attitude of readiness. There are a few vital areas of our personal and professional lives that cannot wait.

Ready to Run

Every step of leadership you take is done with your body. Every message you deliver, every word you type, every task you accomplish, and every meeting you attend is made possible by your body. In fact, everything the Holy Spirit does in and through you involves your body because it is the place where he dwells. "Do you not know that your bodies are temples of the Holy Spirit, who is in you, whom you have received from God?" (1 Corinthians 6:19). It is wise to conclude, then, that the condition of your body will directly impact the effectiveness of your leadership.

I don't want to go so far as to say that we all have to develop athletic bodies hardened by hours of intense exercise every week. I do, however, encourage anyone who wants to lead others to follow a regimen that develops physical stamina, weight control, and mobility.

The human body was made to move. We have been equipped by our Creator with a sturdy skeletal structure, dynamic muscles, strong connecting tissues, and hinged joints. We can walk, run, jump, climb, ride bikes, and grasp implements. It seems obvious that God gave our bodies these capabilities because he wants us to move regularly. Part of being an effective leader is implementing a habitual exercise program. There are a number of inherent benefits to being physically active:

You will be stronger. The more you use your muscles the stronger they get. When you fail to keep these muscles, they atrophy and lose their vitality.

You will feel better about yourself. Exercising naturally releases endorphins into your bloodstream. These powerful chemicals lower your blood pressure and your heart rate. They create a general sense of wellbeing. In addition, your appearance will be more pleasing to you when you look in the mirror.

You will lower your stress level. Exercise tends to sharpen your focus. As you are working out, you will focus on fewer topics, try to solve fewer problems, and give yourself a break from the endless responsibilities of your life. This intensity of focus gives your soul a break and raises your energy level. In addition, the exercise burns off adrenaline and releases emotional energy that has built up.

You will weigh less. Your body has a remarkable ability to survive. When you take in more calories than you burn during the day, your body will store those excess calories as fat. It does this because a mechanism in your body believes you must be stocking up because a crisis is on the horizon. When you commit to be in motion, another trigger kicks into gear. Your body starts to believe it has enough nutrition and is now ready for action. Once you start moving, your body wants to make it easier on you, so it begins to shed pounds. You can accelerate the process by cutting calories, but your body will reward you if you stay in a routine of exercise.

Step by Step

After watching the movie *Aladdin*, a five-year-old kid named Eric started using his mother's empty teakettle as a magic lamp, pretending he could summon the genie and grant wishes. "Make three wishes, Mom," he told his mother, "and I'll make the genie grant them."

His mom first asked to rescue all poor kids from poverty. Eric proceeded to rub "the lamp" and pretended to talk to the invisible genie, then proclaimed his mom's wish fulfilled.

Next, his mom asked for a cure for all sick kids. Again, Eric rubbed the pretend lamp and spoke to the invisible genie, then said his mom's second wish was fulfilled.

Eric's mother then looked down at her own rather ample figure and made her third wish, "I wish to be thin again."

At this Eric started rubbing his magic lamp furiously. When the magic obviously failed to work, Eric looked up at his mom and said very matter-of-factly, "Mom, I think I'm going to need a lot more powerful magic for this wish!" [1]

There is no magic formula, one-step process, or easy program you can follow to maintain good physical health. You can, however, take strategic steps to keep your energy level high and make your body a comfortable place for the Holy Spirit to live.

Consult with your doctor. Exercise is good for you and you need to be smart about it. If you are new to the world of exercise, you want to make sure you start appropriately and that you get clearance from your doctor. Several physical conditions must be taken into account when you design your program. If you are struggling with high blood pressure, diabetes, obesity, joint problems, or a chronic disease, your regimen must account for these and ought to be monitored closely by your physician. If these are not issues for you, it's still a great idea to get the green light from your doctor.

Commit to an exercise routine. We humans are famous for beginning exercise routines only to give up on them when they get boring or difficult. Can I state the obvious? It's going to be difficult and it will be boring at times. We don't live to exercise; we exercise to live. The benefit in your exercise routine is in the fact that it's ongoing. It takes days and days of exercise over several months to train your body to be in shape.

We are privileged in that we have several options for developing a program to get us in the kind of shape we choose to be in. Most of them will work because they are based on sound research about the human body. Therefore, the one that will work for you is the one you like the best and believe will work. You may consider:

- A self-designed workout regimen based on your personal experience.

- A membership in a local gym with personal trainers who can design a program for you.

- Participation in classes where you work out with others.
- A DVD program that you follow in the privacy of your home.
- Recreational classes at your local community college.
- Local clubs that engage in hiking, running, kayaking, or other physical activity.
- An agreement with friends to meet regularly to walk, run, or ride bikes.
- A combination of any of these choices.

Choose a meal plan. If we can get the emotions out of our food decisions, our diets would become simple math problems. We take in calories through the food we eat. We burn calories through the processes that run naturally in our bodies and through the physical activity we engage in. If you burn more than you ingest, you lose weight. If your intake matches your output, your weight remains the same. If you eat more calories than you burn through exercise, you will add weight.

The problem is with our emotional attachment to food. When we eat, many of our senses light up. Our taste buds react to everything we eat. Our olfactory glands create memories from the aromas. It has been shown that meals even trigger different aspects of our brains. For instance, when a man eats, the part of his brain that makes him feel happier is stimulated. When a woman eats the same meal, the part of her brain that sharpens her eyesight is stimulated.

These powerful reactions to food make eating more than sustenance for most of us. We eat to enhance relationships. We eat to relieve stress. We eat to feel pleasure. We eat to reward ourselves. In order to monitor our food intake to maintain a target weight, the plan must include decisions that keep our emotions in check. Decisions are the key because our emotions follow our decisions.

We can think about our emotional response to food and not create any change. Most of us already know it's not good to be overweight. Most of us know we should eat a balanced diet. Most of us know we should exercise moderation when it comes to fried foods and foods high in sugar and fat. Knowing these facts, however, has never changed anyone's life. Choosing consistently to act on this knowledge will create new habits and new results because the decisions focus the emotional energy.

We can also experiment with disciplines without actually making changes. This is why so many of us have been frustrated by various diets. The diets were well-designed and probably had impressive short-term results. Most diets end up not working because they are approached as experiments rather than commitments. We feel good when we start, so we approach it with enthusiasm. Then it turns into a routine and loses its emotional appeal. Rather than push through the boredom to retrain our emotions, we return to the behaviors previously programmed into our souls.

The good news is that our emotional attachment is trainable. We weren't born with a love for specific foods. We developed it over time. Your family raised you with certain foods and traditions. You developed an emotional attachment to these meals and memories that has now programmed you to long for them. Since these are learned responses, you can retrain them. If you remain committed to a disciplined meal plan, you will develop an emotional attachment to the foods you have included. Your soul will fight you at first because it wants to keep its allegiance to past experiences. The struggle may become intense, but then in a breakthrough moment, your attachments will change. You'll begin to discover that your new food choices feel better to you than your old choices.

Your Unique Abilities

You are an incredibly talented person and you work with incredibly talented people. You have been created with at least one unique ability that gives you remarkable potential. Your unique abilities are strong and demand expression. As a result, they are both incredible and inconvenient. When your unique abilities are focused and you express them with humility, they add a lot to your life. When your unique abilities are undisciplined and expressed with selfishness, they are irritating and can even be damaging.

Your unique abilities are so central to who you are that you have no choice but to build your life around them. When you exercise your unique abilities, you feel more like yourself than at any other time. As a result, you are drawn to people who appreciate your unique contribution to life.

Part of your mission is to identify the unique abilities of the people you lead and find ways to utilize those abilities to accomplish your vision. When the people in your charge regularly put their unique abilities into action, everyone is more confident, more positive, and more productive.

People will continue to follow your lead when they feel valued and important around you and believe their abilities can make a contribution to your vision. People also want to be involved in something bigger than themselves, but they don't want to lose their individual identity in the process. For that reason, they look for leaders who have a vision they can believe in. They may not say it, but they also hold the expectation that what they do best will be utilized in the process. They want to help solve problems, add creativity, make decisions, and get things done. When these flow out of their unique ability, the process feels almost effortless as they realize this is what they were made for. When they can't utilize their unique ability, they lose motivation and underachieve.

Remarkable Talents

Since God is a remarkable Creator, you have been "fearfully and wonderfully made" (Psalm 139:14). You are a reflection of his image (Genesis 1:27). As a result, you possess skills and natural talents. In addition, the Spirit of God provides gifts to everyone who has trusted in Christ as Savior (1 Corinthians 12). The result of all this is that you are proficient in some areas while you struggle in others.

The idea of unique abilities is easy to conceptualize but challenging to apply. The concept is that you have been created with natural talents, and when you exercise these natural talents, you are proficient and confident. You enjoy operating in your unique abilities and are highly effective when your talents are being used. The same applies to spiritual gifts. Since they are God-given and empowered by the Holy Spirit, they are effective as they influence others to be stronger and more focused. When your spiritual gift is in action, wisdom flows and the associated tasks seem easy. These thoughts, however, don't tell you how to find your unique abilities or how to apply them in real life.

Finding the Clues to Uniqueness

Your unique ability forms a treasure in you that was designed to make a difference in your world. The problem is that the treasure is hidden. God designed life in such a way that the discovery process is a personal adventure. It's one of the reasons we as a culture are intrigued with movies such as the Indiana Jones series. He searches the earth, deciphers hieroglyphics, and faces down danger to find the treasure that has been hidden for decades.

In the same way, your unique ability requires courage, curiosity, and contemplation on your part to clearly identify what you are best at. It takes this kind of effort because recognizing your unique ability elevates you to a place of high responsibility. When you are aware of what you do better than other people, you can't make excuses to avoid exercising your gift. When you are in touch with your talents, you can't be content with underachieving. Knowing who you are will always motivate you to action.

When we are immature, we tend not to see our giftedness clearly because we are not ready to step into the lifestyle that logically follows. When you are highly stressed, it is often difficult to focus on your giftedness as anxiety steals the energy needed to operate at a high level. We all have sophisticated defenses that protect our hearts when we are not ready for action. Once you are ready to put your unique ability into play, the fog of confusion lifts and possibilities become clear.

Your best decisions, strongest impact, and wisest problem solving happen when you are operating in your unique ability. You don't want to wait until the decision presents itself or the problem arises before you figure out how your unique ability works. That is the point of being ready. You want to identify your talent, read about your talent, practice your talent, make adjustments to how you apply your talent, and talk to others who have a similar mix of abilities as you. As you diligently develop your aptitude, you will increase your influence because you will perform well at the appropriate time.

It Started Young

The discovery process began when you were a child. You became aware that something in you longed to be expressed. It was powerful, so you looked for ways to live it out. It was immature, however, so you were often awkward with it. The world was cruel, so you were criticized and made fun of as you tried to discover who you were and how you were supposed to impact the world.

Some of you faced the challenge with thick skin and ignored most of the criticism. You have grown in confidence as you pushed through the barriers to your development. Some of you were much more sensitive to the ridicule. You felt crushed as a child, and you are still struggling to find your place. You are afraid to explore new possibilities because the criticism is still fresh in your soul. You would rather just do what you are comfortable with because it's safe, even if it's boring.

As an adult, peer pressure is less of an issue and productivity has become a much greater motivator. You probably have a family to provide for, workers who depend upon you, and a desire to make a contribution to your career field. These factors cause you to get busy exploring ways to make a living. In the process, you gain life experience, which helps clarify who you are.

There has never been anyone with the exact collection of wisdom, talents, and intuition that you naturally possess. There is, therefore, no list of unique abilities that you can choose from to identify what you are best at. Instead, you are on a journey that will unfold a piece at a time as you gradually discover both your talents and your purpose. Although there is no list of unique talents, they do operate in categories. Your unique ability is a combination of traits taken from these categories.

Category 1: Physical Aptitudes

You are a physical being made up of bones, muscles, connecting tissue, and nerves. The activities of your body are coordinated by your brain, the most sophisticated computer in the world. The brain constantly sends impulses to the rest of your body instructing it in both voluntary and involuntary movements. As your mind organizes your movements, you discover that you are really good at some things while you are all thumbs at others.

Some of you are great with today's do-it-yourself trend. You like to build and repair things. You are even amazed at your ability to figure out unique solutions to physical challenges. Some of you are naturally talented in small-motor skills. You may be a crafter or technician with dexterity in sewing, knitting, quilting, or manufacturing. You may be a professional who uses your gentle touch in surgery or in the production of delicate electronic equipment. You have a steady hand and can navigate intricate movements with skill. Your touch might be used in applying makeup, massage, or the decorative flair. When others attempt to do what you do easily, they destroy the very thing they are trying to fix or create. What you find easy, they find impossible.

Others of you are natural at sports and physical activities such as dance or movement. Your confidence on the playing field gives you confidence in life. Being in shape seems the only way to live, and while others avoid things that make them sweat, your life feels empty without such exertion.

Some of you, unfortunately, should avoid home repairs, manufacturing tasks, and anything requiring physical dexterity at all costs. You will inevitably make things worse every time you touch a tool, and every attempt to save money by doing it yourself ends up costing a lot more as you hire people to fix your mistakes.

Category 2: Wisdom and Insight

Our minds work incredibly well. They put together thoughts and make conclusions. Some of you, however, have an unusual ability to understand certain areas of life. You may have insight into business practices that make complex processes simple. You may have wisdom about decision making that gives you the ability to coach others in their pursuits. You may have understanding about financial operations that make you an adept investor or financial advisor.

If this is your unique ability, you have moments of clarity that are astounding. As you converse with others, the next course of action becomes crystal clear. You can see the issues, the obstacles, and the way to navigate the course ahead. The path is so clear you can confidently lead people through. You may even become impatient with those who question your conclusions because the solution is just so evident to you.

On a personal level, you gain insight into God's plan for your life as you exercise your gifts. As you serve others, you discover that much of what you do for others applies to you also. You become one of the people who benefits from the exercise of your gifts.

I was talking recently with a man whose gifts are in leadership and exhortation. We talked about business issues and the relationships that help build a healthy career. "It's amazing how much productivity gets lost because of problems at home," he said. "I've noticed in my own home that my wife sets the atmosphere for the whole family." We started talking about the impact of our marriages on our productivity, and he said, "When I get home, I'm going to make it my first goal to help my wife feel secure with me. I bet that will help with everything."

He had just given himself advice that he was confident was the right course to take. That's how it works. As you use your gift to help others, God will highlight areas of your relationship that will make a big difference.

Category 3: Technology

We live in a highly technological age. It's hard to believe that so much of our life is controlled by very fast moving ones and zeros! Our lives are enhanced by computers, smartphones, portable media players, digital cable, global positioning devices, the digital cloud, and home entertainment systems. The pace of growth in technology is so fast, however, that we can only imagine the technological wonders the future will hold for us.

In the midst of relentless electronic development, you may be someone who has unusual understanding of how all of this works. Computers are straightforward for you. The interconnection between computer networks, cell phones, and portable devices makes sense to you. When new technology appears, it doesn't take you long to figure it out and put it into action.

You may even have a high aptitude for programming as well as setting up and troubleshooting devices. We are all grateful to you for providing the rest of us with the technological advances we count on. Most of us could never do what you do. It doesn't take long for us to be completely overwhelmed when you explain to us how technology works at its most basic level.

You may be very good at helping others interface with technology. You accept that much of technology is a foreign language to most people who need to use it in their work or personal lives. You are able to explain procedures to us in simple terms we can understand. You are helping to make complex computer systems user-friendly so they can have widespread applications.

Category 4: Relationships

Perhaps you have strong natural instincts for the way relationships work. You sense people's moods and needs. You seem to have an innate ability to know when people need a little bit of your time or a lot of your time to resolve issues. You also creatively come up with ways to communicate that encourage and inspire others.

Some of you have relationship skills for the everyday interaction of friendship. You are adept at staying in touch with people through email, social media, phone conversations, and personal meetings. You know what is happening in people's lives, and you regularly encourage them in their pursuits.

Others of you are talented in coaching others in their relationships. Perhaps you first noticed this in your teen years when your friends consistently came to you for advice. You didn't really understand why they came to you, but you seemed to have answers for them. As an adult, you have been helping people figure out their relationships in a combination of casual and formal settings. Your friends probably call you for advice. You may be leading a Bible study or prayer group that focuses on the important relationships in one another's lives.

Some of you with this ability are helping others heal. You are probably a people helper by profession or you help lead a recovery ministry in your community. As others share their stories, you have an uncanny ability to see the path that will lead them away from their pain toward healthy decisions. You get burdened by the number of painful stories you hear, but you cannot escape the insight you have to promote healing in people's hearts.

This is a part of my unique ability. Since graduating from seminary, I have spent countless hours studying how relationships work, helping people work through relational issues, and brainstorming ways to communicate practical relationship principles.

Category 5: Musical Talent

Music is a powerful force in our lives. Music stirs the heart, ignites our emotions, and engages our imaginations. It has the ability to connect our thoughts, emotions, and actions to inspire us to better things in life.

Some of you have been gifted with musical talent for the benefit of the rest of us. You can play and sing on-key. Your voice is equipped to sing. Musical instruments make sense to you, and the study of music is fascinating to you. You may be gifted in playing or singing or composing. You may enjoy the stage or the solitude of a studio, but you love music and are good at expressing yourself in song.

This is definitely not part of my unique ability. When I became a youth pastor, I decided to learn how to play the guitar. I enjoyed playing, but I grew frustrated because I couldn't tell when my guitar was out of tune. Well, that's not entirely true. I knew something was wrong from the grimaces of many in the audience.

Category 6: Creative Arts

Creative expression is one of the great gifts of life. It has given rise to drama, fine art, movies, television, home décor, and graphic art. If you have this gift, life makes sense to you in a way the average person doesn't comprehend. You see shapes, colors, and concepts with unusual clarity and beauty. When you express yourself, other people experience aha moments. They look at your work and say, "That's incredible." They ask you to create a logo but can't explain what it should look like, only how they want it to feel. When you give the feeling a shape, they say to you, "That's it! How did you come up with that?" You can't really answer their question because the idea just occurred to you, and you knew it was right.

Category 7: Leadership

Most of you reading this book are probably natural born leaders. You seem to rise to leadership in everything you've ever been involved with. Your peers have chosen you to lead since childhood. Your ideas are respected, and your directions are generally put into action. You have noticed that some people try to lead, but others do not follow. You, on the other hand, always have a following, even when you wish you could be left alone.

My wife, Pam, has this skill set. Decision making is natural for her. She has written books such as *Woman of Influence, Becoming a Brave New Woman,* and *The 10 Best Decisions a Woman Can Make* because setting the pace for women is in her soul. Her love for ministering to couples and families grows out of her love to help women succeed in their most vital relationships. Because she is a visionary, a leader, and a decision maker, she needs a spouse who can flex and adapt as she changes course, sets plans in place, and moves through life at a frenetic pace. She needs a team around her to follow up and follow through on the plans she sets in motion.

Our oldest son, Brock, also has a unique ability to lead groups in competitive settings. I recently sat in on a football team meeting he ran. Every player was given a scouting report for the upcoming game. As Brock went over the report, he broke their assignments down into simple steps with familiar terminology. It was clear that he had spent weeks building a common language for the program. He used phrases such as "5 x 5" and "shade technique." I didn't know what these meant, but the players obviously did. When they left the room, all the players knew what they were supposed to do and had confidence they could do it.

Category 8: Communication

You may have unusual skill in communicating life principles to other people. Others listen to you and say, "Yeah, that's what I've been thinking, but I didn't know how to say it." You may prefer private conversations in which you share with friends your perspective on life or you may seek out opportunities to present in front of groups. You may be drawn to teaching as a profession or you may be interested in public speaking. You may even discover that you have a knack for communication over public airwaves so that radio or television broadcasting is an attractive venture for you. In any case, you have a way with words that makes complex principles easy for the average person to digest.

Category 9: Finances

In elementary school, you might have read about a mythological character named Midas—everything he touched turned to gold. Some of you have that touch. You love finances, and you are good at making and keeping money. You love the rush of making the deal or watching interest accumulate. A balanced Excel spreadsheet warms your heart.

People with this gift often lead very busy lives. They may be corporate executives or entrepreneurs, but no matter the title, the hours can be long. The spouse married to a person with this Midas touch needs to value being married to someone God entrusts resources to because they've proven themselves to be a good steward.

Collect the Evidence

Grade yourself on a 0–5 scale for each of the categories in the chart below. A score of 0 means you have no measurable talent in that area. A 5 means you are highly proficient in that arena.

Unique Ability Category	Score
Physical Aptitudes	
Wisdom and Insight	
Technology	
Relationships	
Musical Talent	
Creative Arts	
Leadership	
Communication	
Finances	

For every category you marked with a 4 or 5, take the following steps:

- Review a book, magazine, Internet article, or podcast that will help you grow in this area.

- Identify someone who is also talented in this area. Make an appointment to ask them how they developed this skill in their life.

- Increase by one hour per week the amount of time you spend working in this area.

- Pray the prayer below inserting your unique abilities into the blanks.

Strategic Prayer

I know that I was created with (insert your unique abilities here) so that I can be highly effective in my life. I was fearfully and wonderfully made when I was in the womb (Psalm 139:14). I am talented and my unique abilities of (insert your unique abilities here) are designed to be fully utilized. I am your workmanship, God, created in Christ Jesus for good works that I should walk in them (Ephesians 2:10). The people I lead are also talented so I can help them succeed without sacrificing my own success (Hebrews 10:24-25). I also realize it's always good to do the right thing and that no true success can come from doing the wrong thing (1 Peter 2:15). I, therefore, commit to do good to those I lead by encouraging them daily as long as it is called today (Hebrews 3:13). Jesus, give me wisdom to energize all the unique abilities that exist in my organization. Amen.

CHAPTER 4

Decide to Be Real

It started out like any other day. The alarm went off at the normal time. Pete got out of bed, had his first cup of coffee, and got ready for work. He and his colleagues started their daily pursuits like any other normal working day. But this day turned out to be a frustrating one. They worked diligently, but circumstances didn't cooperate very well, so the results were unimpressive. They spent more time on maintenance and practicing their skills than on achieving any measurable goal.

Then, without any preplanning, a local preacher asked to borrow Pete's vehicle so he could stand on it and deliver an impromptu sermon. Pete liked this preacher, and since he had nothing better going on this day, he agreed. After the sermon was over, this unassuming preacher challenged Pete and his colleagues to go back to work and do exactly what they had been doing all day long.

You can almost hear Pete's thoughts. *This preacher borrows my work vehicle and now he thinks he's an expert at what I do for a living. What a waste of time! But there's an audience, and if I blow off this man, it will affect my reputation. If I take his advice, I'll be throwing away a couple of hours, which I don't want to do, but I guess I have no choice.*

Reluctantly, Peter, James, and John loaded up their nets, got back in their boats, and went out to the same waters where they had caught nothing earlier. But when they let down the nets, "they caught such a large number of fish that their nets began to break" (Luke 5:6).

Suddenly, life had changed. The man they thought was just a local preacher proved he had authority over nature. Peter's self-confidence quickly became self-awareness: "Go away from me, Lord; I am a sinful man!" (5:8). Their careers were transformed with a single statement, "Don't be afraid; from now on you will fish for people" (5:10). Before they could even process the magnitude of what had just happened, "they pulled their boats up on shore, left everything and followed him" (5:11)

Get Used to Things Happening Quickly

As a leader, you are probably hard working, enthusiastic, and determined to make something happen in your world. The rest of us count on you for this as we gain confidence from your forward thinking and can-do attitude. At the same time, there is only so much you can do. In your ability to achieve, you are still limited. In your influence, you can move people only so far. We all know this, so we look for leaders who are real. We want leaders who see life as it really is and deal with their own humanity honestly while they also believe in the effectiveness of their leadership.

A big part of being real is accepting that at any time, at any moment, your life can change. God has sovereign control over our lives, so any day could be the time when a breakthrough takes place, a setback forges new character, or your purpose finds new clarity.

As I look back on my life, the biggest steps have happened quickly. I simply went to a movie at the age of sixteen and was confronted with my need for a Savior. I faithfully went to a leadership conference at nineteen, having no idea I was going to meet my life partner. On an otherwise uneventful day, I heard the words, "We are going to be parents!" I asked Jim Conway to mentor me as a pastor, having no idea that one day, out of the blue, he would challenge Pam and me to become authors. At a simple visit to the doctor's office for a sinus infection, I was asked, "How long have you had high blood pressure?"

These moments changed my life quickly and unexpectedly. It

was impossible at the beginning of each of those days to predict how important they would become, but each one led to key decisions and sweeping adjustments in my life. Today could be one of those days. Of course, today could just be another routine day of getting ready for one of those days. Either way, being real means we will live today with patient anticipation. We will faithfully carry out our leadership responsibilities today, but we remain willing to respond quickly the next time Jesus makes a change in our lives.

What Really Matters to You

Leadership puts us in situations that expose our character, and often we don't get to plan when those situations occur. Somebody walks into your office with a problem that requires your full focus. You get a financial report that short-circuits your plans. You experience sudden success that raises people's expectations of you. Moments like these force your priorities and personal character to the surface and reveal what you are really made of.

When life is easy and stress free, you can carry out a role and act properly. When stress is high and interruptions are intense, the real you comes to the forefront. One of the most strategic questions a leader can ask then is, "Who am I really? When the pressure is on, what will end up being truly important to me?"

In Acts 24, Paul had an opportunity to talk with Felix, the governor, several times about the most important issues of life. Because Felix was married to a Jewish woman, he was interested in Jewish things and wondered why this new movement, then called "the Way," was so popular. In their interactions, Paul spoke about three main themes that reflected timeless truths—truths that shaped who he was and the purpose to which he gave his time, resources, and focus: "As Paul talked about righteousness, self-control and the judgment to come, Felix was afraid and said, 'That's enough for now! You may leave. When I find it convenient, I will send for you'" (24:25).

Righteousness. This is not the righteousness born out of self-effort, which says, "I will try harder to be better than I am." It's the righteousness given to us when we trust in Christ as our Savior. It is the ability of the Holy Spirit in us producing behavior that is beyond our natural ability.

The picture that sticks in my mind is riding jet skis on the Colorado River with my sons. I was on the back while Caleb, who was fifteen at the time, drove. He pushed the throttle wide open and propelled us along the surface of the water at sixty-five miles per hour. All I could do was hold on and hope it went well. It occurred to me as we rocketed along, *I could never swim this fast. No matter how hard I tried or how much training I engaged in, it would be impossible for me on my own to travel this fast on the water. But with this machine under us, it was easy.*

True righteousness is the power of the Holy Spirit working in us, making it easy to do what otherwise would be impossible.

Self-control. This is the fruit of the Spirit that enables us to say no to what is unhealthy, yes to what is healthy, and "I will stay at it" with our commitments. We are filled with passions by our maker so that we will pursue aggressive, energetic lives. Without self-control, these passions become misdirected and destructive. Most of human history is the story of people who could not, or would not, rein in their hunger for power, sexual passions, or addictive behaviors. Most of them started out with a desire to build something worthwhile, but they ended up with empty lives and failed relationships. True success can be achieved only by steering the powerful passions of life with self-control.

The judgment to come. The great equalizer of life is the end event when we all stand before our Creator to give an account. It should not come as a surprise. We all answer to parents, teachers, or bosses. Without leadership, everything moves toward chaos. In the same way, without a life referee, all things would grow chaotic and hurtful. Jesus is faithful and will hold court at the end of our lives to settle all accounts and hand out either rewards or consequences. Those who believe this will actually happen happily evaluate their lives along the way. Those who deny this will happen let the imaginations of their hearts run wild. Somebody needs to be the referee. I'm glad it is the Creator who sees all.

How about you? What are the truly important issues that guide you as a leader? What are the subjects you find yourself talking about often? What topics cause you to be upset when they get challenged or hindered?

Respect the Power

Leaders who are committed to be real recognize that we were created with inherent power. Our words can heal emotional wounds, motivate people to action, frustrate people's efforts, or educate others toward excellence. Our decisions can guide movements or cause momentum to deteriorate. Our moral decisions can give others the courage to live healthy or they can create damage to families, careers, friendships, and personal contentment.

I used to think of verses like "I will be careful to lead a blameless life" (Psalm 101:2) as a call to noble self-discipline that would prevent me from being embarrassed when I met Jesus face-to-face. Then I traveled to Germany and rode on the autobahn. We were tooling along at a comfortable 120 miles per hour when a Porsche 911 Turbo blew by us as if we were standing still. What a rush! It stimulated my soul with sights, sounds, and emotions. It felt like a predator stalking its prey when I caught a glimpse of the silver vehicle approaching in the mirror. It was like a flash of lightning as it shot past us. There was something primal about the roar of the engine and the whine of the turbocharger as it outdistanced us so quickly we could hardly take in the experience. I thought, *Whoa, that was awesome. I wish I could be in that driver's seat. It must be a rush to go that fast with that much horsepower at your fingertips.*

When we later passed the same vehicle, my thoughts were quite different. Somehow that car had gotten out of control, causing a violent accident. I could still see pieces of silver sheet metal, but the car was barely recognizable. Parts were strewn across the road and into the surrounding fields, and fire and smoke billowed from the wreckage. Rescue personnel were on the scene, but you could tell from their demeanor that this driver had experienced his last great run. Everyone else on the road was reduced to slow speeds as officials took control of the scene. The power that was so impressive less than an hour before had now created dramatic damage.

My thoughts were different this time: *That was one powerful machine. I guess the driver should have paid closer attention. When you're running fast, it doesn't take much to turn a thrill ride into a disaster.*

The inherent power of our lives is the real reason we must all be careful how we live. We are much more like that Porsche than any of us realize. We have more influence on more people than we will ever be aware of. If we ever accept that our lives are impressively equipped and remarkably capable, we will pay close attention to how we live. We will view David's thoughts in Psalm 101 as a driver's manual for life:

- I will conduct the affairs of my house with a blameless heart (v. 2).

- I will not look with approval on anything that is vile (v. 3).

- I hate what faithless people do; I will have no part in it (v. 3).

- I will have nothing to do with what is evil (v. 4).

- Whoever has haughty eyes and a proud heart, I will not tolerate (v. 5).

- My eyes will be on the faithful in the land (v. 6).

- The one whose walk is blameless will minister to me (v. 6).

- No one who practices deceit will dwell in my house (v. 7).

If, however, we assume our lives are small and our actions don't really affect anyone else, we will live carelessly. Just about every week of my life I hear a story of someone who miscalculated the power of their lives. They thought their actions didn't matter. They assumed no one would get hurt. They refused to believe their lives were highly influential. Then that moment happened when they got out of control and the crash was awful.

A realistic view of your life will lead you to respect the power.

Course Corrections

Leadership involves guiding people in the pursuit of a vision by accomplishing strategic goals. In the process, individuals, groups, and organizations occasionally get off track. Sometimes people get off track out of sincere effort. They are trying to do their best, but they reach incorrect conclusions. At other times, they are stubborn or proud and deliberately attempt to take over the direction of the organization. In either case, real leaders recognize the tendency of people to lose focus on the goal and are willing to make midcourse corrections to bring them back.

Paul wrote the book of Galatians because some good friends in the province of Galatia had gotten off track with the thing that was most important to him. To get their attention, he responded with strong words: "But even if we or an angel from heaven should preach a gospel other than the one we preached to you, let them be under God's curse!" (1:8). Obviously, the gospel was the most important thing in Paul's life and rightly so. The gospel had saved him from himself and from a terrible eternity. He relied on it heavily because:

- It gave him his purpose: "Paul, an apostle—sent not from men nor by a man, but by Jesus Christ" (v. 1).

- It was powerful enough to give him direction because it was made possible by "God the Father, who raised [Christ] from the dead" (v. 1).

- It was selflessly secured by Christ "who gave himself for our sins" (v. 4).

- It provided security in an insecure world because it "rescues us from the present evil age" (v. 4).

- It set people free (including Paul) by "the one who called you to live in the grace of Christ" (v. 6).

Paul had experienced a transformation through a relationship with Christ. He went from persecuting the church to proclaiming the very message he tried to silence. He went from being bound to a long list of "have tos" to being free to pursue a whole world of "get tos." He went from a pursuit of misguided self-effort to a God-given purpose empowered by the Holy Spirit. It shaped his life, settled his attitude, and satisfied his soul despite the difficulties involved. It was so effective that he would accept no substitutes. Instead, it drove him to make corrections in his life and challenge those he led to alter their course when necessary.

What areas of your responsibility require an intense awareness of when corrections are needed? I agree with Paul that the good news of the death and resurrection of Jesus is the most important message on earth. I would also say that the day I met Jesus when I was sixteen years old was the most formative day of my life. It awakened something in me I didn't even know existed. It shaped the direction of my life and planted in me the desire to pursue ministry as my main focus. So much so that when my ministry is not progressing the way I would like, I get frustrated. A restlessness sets in that must be addressed. My mind dwells on what must be done to get things back in motion. My emotions churn within me until a solution can be found that makes it possible to operate at full speed. Lower priorities get ignored to make room for commitments that will reenergize the higher concern.

Every leader I know does the same thing. The content of their guiding vision may be different from mine, but they protect it with the same intensity. They pursue it with the same zeal. They plan their lives around it with the same determination. They push it regardless of the cost to themselves, the peace of their relationships, or their personal health.

Being real means you seek to be aware of these areas so you don't overreact. We are all emotionally attached to our areas of leadership, so it's not uncommon for us to get angry, scared, disappointed, or just plain frantic when things are neglected or distorted from their original plan. The big questions then are, "What is your top leadership priority? Is it worth holding on to? Is it powerful enough to make proper course corrections in your personal life and your leadership responsibilities?" When the answer is no, change is in order. When the answer is yes, it becomes a powerful force to build your confidence and expand your influence.

Real Leaders Serve

One of the great concepts of Christian living is servanthood. Jesus said, "The greatest among you will be your servant" (Matthew 23:11). It sounds good and noble, but it has some rough implications. Servants respond to the initiative of their masters. Servants live for the good of other people. Servants make sacrifices that benefit others.

As I consider this, I cannot escape the conclusion that much of what I go through in life is not personal. I told God years ago that I wanted to be a servant of his. I didn't know all that was involved in that commitment, but I sincerely meant it. I have since learned that God takes his servants through many experiences so that later we can relate to others who have been through similar experiences. Many of the hardships, corrections, challenges, and blessings are there as training. They are not in response to anything we have or haven't done.

Real servants embrace a selfless process of commitment by repeatedly asking two questions:

- What are the greatest needs of those I lead?

- What is the best thing in my power to do to help meet these needs?

This was the approach Jesus took. He looked at the needs of mankind and concluded that our most important need was forgiveness. He was aware of our need for basic necessities, companionship, financial provision, and personal growth. He knew, however, that these needs paled in comparison to our need to be forgiven so we could receive eternal salvation as a gift of grace. He decided to give his life, therefore, as the necessary sacrifice. He suffered, but it wasn't because of anything he had done. He humbled himself, but it wasn't because he had a personal need to do so. He accepted criticism and accusations without answering back, not because he had done anything wrong, but because we needed a Savior.

This is a tough principle to imitate. When things are difficult, I easily get introspective and conclude the setbacks must be the result of a lack of talent, perspective, or maturity. To be sure, I make my share of mistakes, so sometimes I earn the right to be disciplined, but it is often not the case. I intellectually accept that God is working to equip me to help others, so I have started praying differently: *Jesus, I'm going to assume that challenges I face are for the purpose of training and they are for the benefit of others. Give me the wisdom to recognize when the hard things in my life are truly about my behavior or attitude. Also, give me the willingness to be an example to others of your justice and grace.*

Tempted to Take Shortcuts

It's tempting when you're trying to move people forward to take shortcuts that conserve energy and resources. There's certainly nothing wrong with taking a more efficient path to the accomplishment of a goal as long as it doesn't ignore key elements. But servants do all the work *that is necessary* even when it's inconvenient or inefficient.

Jesus set the standard for us when it comes to temptation: "For we do not have a high priest who is unable to empathize with our weaknesses, but we have one who has been tempted in every way, just as we are—yet he did not sin" (Hebrews 4:15). When I first read this verse, I have to admit that I thought, *That's not possible. He's God and I certainly am not. Most of my temptations seem petty and self-serving. There's no way Jesus was tempted like that.*

I have since taken great comfort in the fact that my Savior is real. He knows what it's like to live a real human life with all its challenges. One of the temptations he faced that gives him clear understanding into our lives is the temptation to follow a shortcut when the full journey is necessary.

Luke 4 contains the synopsis of Jesus's forty days of temptation in the wilderness. I'm sure there were more than three instances during this time when Satan attempted to knock Jesus off stride, but these three summarize the enemy's tactics, and they all include a shortcut.

> The devil said to him, "If you are the Son of God, tell this stone to become bread" (Luke 4:3).

Certainly Jesus was hungry, but there was also a commonly held belief that the Messiah would bring something like manna when he appeared to set Israel free. Jesus is being told, "If you turn these stones into bread, we can take care not only of your need to eat, but we can announce who you really are and get on with the program."

> The devil...showed him...all the kingdoms of the world. And he said to him, "I will give you all their authority and splendor; it has been given to me, and I can give it to anyone I want to. If you worship me, it will all be yours" (4:5-7).

Satan had wrestled dominion over the world away from Adam in the original temptation; now he's offering it to Jesus. He's telling Jesus, "I know your plan is to be the ruler of all, and I know a way to give that to you without you having to go to the cross. You don't have to sacrifice yourself. I can give it to you now!"

This is where the temptation to shortcut the process is clearest. Satan could have delivered on this. Jesus could legitimately have taken over as the ruler of the world, but he would have been leading non-redeemed people forever. The cycle of death would go on perpetually because there would be no solution for the sin of mankind. The old nature of man would be an eternal struggle because the process of the new birth would never have been instituted. Jesus knew that the long path was the only way to fulfill the plan.

> The devil led him to Jerusalem and had him stand on the highest point of the temple. "If you are the Son of God," he said, "throw yourself down from here" (4:9).

Satan changed his tactic at this point and said, "Okay, since you are determined to walk through the plan, how about we get the show started? If you want people to know who you are so you can become their Messiah, let's have you jump from the top of the temple so angels can help you make a miraculous landing. After all, you never get a second chance to make a first impression. Let's go big!"

Jesus could certainly have pulled this off, but he knew that too much attention too soon would short-circuit his goal. It was going to take time to train his followers and establish his credentials beyond doubt.

The greatest work to ever take place on earth was going to take time. Jesus was smart enough at twelve to begin his public ministry, but he waited until he was thirty. He was powerful enough at thirty to sacrifice himself, but he took three years to train his disciples so they could succeed as apostles.

Shortcuts can be a great asset, but they are no substitute for finishing the race.

Carried Away

Being real means admitting that we are all prone to the self-centered and self-absorbed conclusion that our lives are the most important, most dramatic topic around. The truth is, we are all part of a worldwide, history-wide story being orchestrated by God himself. As a result, some remarkable things happen that involve us because we are a reflection of the image of God. Everyone around us, however, is just as likely to be doing remarkable feats with God's help. This is why humility is such an important ingredient in the life of a leader. Humility says, "Of course I'm very good at some things because God is working in me. Similarly, others are very good at some things because God is also at work in them. I rejoice that God is at work!"

I'm still reeling from a family I met recently. I was performing a simple wedding followed by a reception at the new couple's home. I sat down to eat lunch with what looked like a very ordinary family. Much to my surprise, they revealed that for fun, they hunt bears! They have a pack of dogs trained to pursue a bear and drive him into a tree. The hunters then approach their prey. They don't hunt with guns, however. They shoot the animal with cameras. They are like the wilderness paparazzi, and they have some of the most dramatic photos I have ever seen. They position themselves within ten to twelve feet of these powerful animals so they can get pictures of them in their natural habitat.

I asked one of them, "Aren't you afraid the bear might jump out of the tree and maul you?"

"Oh, the dogs would never let that happen," he said.

I felt small yet inspired. I have enjoyed some great experiences, but I have never done anything like this. I now know, however, that it's possible. And that's the point. Big things are possible because we all have a big God living in us who has power, knowledge, courage, focus, and an adventurous spirit. In the right way, getting carried away in life is to be expected because God regularly does what is beyond our imagination.

Muddy Tires

Every once in a while I hear a statement that captures my attention and gets my mind racing. It happened recently with one of my sons. He has taken up mountain biking as a hobby and decided to explore a new trail. It had snowed a couple of weeks before, and temperatures had been fluctuating from midtwenties at night to high forties during the day. He researched the trail on the Internet and carefully planned his route. He didn't take into account, however, that the slowly melting snow would affect the trail. I asked him how his ride went.

"I didn't get very far," he said. "So much mud accumulated in my tires that they stopped moving. I had to pick mud and rocks out of the tread. I finally had to just turn around, find a hose, and ride home on the streets."

We laughed about it as he told the story, but the idea that accumulated mud stopped his progress wouldn't go away. It reminded me that real leaders expect obstacles and develop a plan to overcome them. Consider some of the ways this applies to our lives.

Life is intricate, so it's hard to predict every obstacle. I may set goals, plan a course of action, anticipate the challenges, and still miss an important fact (such as melting snow creating mud). Remaining flexible enough to make midcourse corrections is as important as being firmly committed.

In this world, mud accumulates. When it's a little, it's not too difficult to deal with. "If we confess our sins, he is faithful and just and will forgive us our sins and purify us from all unrighteousness" (1 John 1:9). We can hose off and get back on the trail without too much effort or agony.

When a lot of mud gums up the works of my life, I must make significant decisions and apply concerted effort. "Come near to God and he will come near to you. Wash your hands, you sinners, and purify your hearts, you double-minded" (James 4:8). If my son had stubbornly kept going, he would have had a very long day. He could have dug the mud out of his tires, rode a few feet, and then repeated the process, but it would have needlessly exhausted him. He could have gotten off and pushed his bike along the trail, but it would have defeated the purpose of trail riding. He could have gotten angry and put more effort into his peddling, but it would have only worn him out without producing any better results. The best thing for my son to do was to turn around, learn from the misadventure, and be wiser next time.

Leaders go backward in their influence when they stubbornly refuse to make changes when mud gets in their tires. We all battle with desires in our hearts that lead us to unproductive and unhealthy paths. We all hit obstacles despite our best intentions. We all face decisions that could needlessly complicate our lives and halt our progress. So often, we just keep moving in the same direction rather than admitting the mistake and turning around, which can create some embarrassing moments.

> After twenty-five years in the same parish, Father O'Shaunessey was saying his farewells at his retirement dinner. An eminent member of the congregation—a leading politician—had been asked to make a presentation and a short speech, but was late arriving.
>
> So the priest took it upon himself to fill the time, and stood up to the microphone:
>
> "I remember the first confession I heard here twenty-five years ago and it worried me as to what sort of place I'd come to...That first confession remains the worst I've ever

heard. The chap confessed that he'd stolen a TV set from a neighbour and lied to the police when questioned...He said that he'd stolen money from his parents and from his employer; that he'd had affairs with several of his friends' wives; that he'd taken hard drugs...You can imagine what I thought...However I'm pleased to say that as the days passed I soon realized that this sad fellow was a frightful exception and that this parish was indeed a wonderful place full of kind and decent people..."

At this point the politician arrived and apologized for being late. He immediately stepped up to the microphone and pulled his speech from his pocket:

"I'll always remember when Father O'Shaunessey first came to our parish," said the politician, "In fact, I'm pretty certain that I was the first person in the parish that he heard in confession."[1]

Relentless

The presence of obstacles also leads to the need for unrelenting persistence as we outlast the storms that seek to disrupt our plans. During a weekend conference Pam and I led in New England, the weather, the schedule, and the people were all relentless. Friday night brought torrential rain. The kind that blurs the lines on the road, turns paths into puddles, and soaks your clothes in an instant. Saturday ushered in showers throughout the day that required rain gear to move anywhere outside.

The conference schedule didn't alter at all because of the rain. We had to move boxes from the car to the building in the rain on Friday night. We had to dash to our car after setup as buckets of water poured over us. The organizer of the event told us before we left, "We never let weather dictate what we're going to do. We'll open the doors earlier tomorrow than we planned so people can get out of the weather, but we'll stay on schedule!"

And the people showed up. They were eager to learn and full of questions. Every free moment was spent meeting with people, answering their inquiries, and helping them make decisions about resources that would help them become stronger people.

"Let us not become weary in doing good, for at the proper time we will reap a harvest if we do not give up" (Galatians 6:9) is a watchword for leaders. My life, like yours, is filled with daily chores, mundane tasks, and challenges that must be overcome. Leadership fills our lives with difficult tasks, relentless problems, persistent criticism, and needy people. One of the most important traits of leaders, therefore, is a relentless will to keep going.

- When you are tired, keep going.
- When you are discouraged, keep going.
- When people disappoint you, keep going.
- When you experience success, keep going.
- When you accomplish a big goal, keep going.
- When you come up short on a pursuit, keep going.
- When someone else gets credit for what you accomplished, keep going.

The world needs the real you—the hard-working, courageous, intense, inherently powerful, ever-adjusting, humbly honest, persistent you.

CHAPTER 5

Decide to Team Up

A few years ago at the Seattle Special Olympics, nine contestants, all physically or mentally disabled, assembled at the starting line for the 100 yard dash. At the gun, they all started out, not exactly in a dash, but with a relish to run the race to the finish and win. All, that is, except one boy who stumbled on the asphalt, tumbled over a couple of times and began to cry. The other eight heard the boy. They slowed down and looked back. They all turned around and went back. Every one of them. One girl with Down's Syndrome bent down and kissed him and said, "This will make it better." All nine linked arms and walked across the finish line together. Everyone in the stadium stood, and the cheering went on for several minutes. People who were there are still telling the story. Why? Because deep down we know one thing. What matters most in this life is more than winning for ourselves. What truly matters in this life is helping others win, even if it means slowing down and changing our course. [1]

We Are Not Alone

Leadership means you are part of a team. If you were acting alone, there would be no need to lead anyone else. We form teams because there are goals we want to pursue that cannot be accomplished on our own. We may need financial resources beyond our own, a talent pool that exceeds our personal talent level, or the job may simply be too big for one person to accomplish. In these situations, a team is necessary, but there are different types of teams and they all have different needs.

To lead a team, therefore, you must first define what type of team you prefer to run. I grew up playing football and basketball. My wife grew up competing in gymnastics and swimming. We were drawn to these competitions because of our personalities and preferences. We were both on teams, but they were quite different from one another.

The four most common types of teams are:

Interdependent Teams. These teams are similar to football, basketball, or any other pursuit that involves team members who work in concert toward a common goal. In this case, each member has a role to play that interacts with the roles of every other member, forming a coordinated effort. The goal of interdependent teams is for many people to work together as if they were one.

Individualized Teams. These teams are similar to a swim team where individuals compete in their own events, but they combine points together as a team. They don't have a big need to coordinate their efforts because they act independently from one another and have individualized goals. As a team, their goal is to show up at the same time so they can "pool" their points.

Intermittent Teams. This would be a team that comes together to run a campaign or event. Political campaigns, fund-raising campaigns, and special events are all examples of intermittent teams. They have a clear starting date, a clear ending date, and a narrow scope.

Interrelated Teams. This is a collection of individuals or groups who work together on specific aspects of their pursuits. Two common examples are farming co-ops and missionary efforts. Farmers often work together to create opportunities to distribute their goods or to negotiate market rates. Churches work together to support missionaries and provide workers for missionary projects. These pursuits are ongoing, but they are limited to specific aspects of operation.

Although every team is unique, all proficient teams adhere to a few common characteristics that enable them to operate at their peak. Without these qualities, a group of people may be working together but a high-performance team is not formed. Teams that function far beyond the sum of their parts will have an inspiring vision, mutual core values, and a clear operational plan.

Inspiring Vision

All teams function best when they have a sense of purpose that is big, challenging, and audacious. In the absence of a clear vision that captures the participants' imagination, the team will naturally turn its focus on itself. Relationships between team members and individual needs become paramount. Since people's needs are unpredictable, pervasive, and inherently self-centered, putting the focus on internal relationships creates a very difficult environment for continual motivation and success. A vision that takes people beyond themselves tends to minimize self-focus, remove obstacles, and create cooperative alliances. The vision helps people answer the questions that determine their attitude toward the pursuit. These questions are:

- Why are we doing this?
- Do we really have to work together?
- What is my role?
- How will I know when we have succeeded?
- Is this worth my best effort?
- Is it worth it to count on others?

Interdependent Teams and Vision

Interdependent teams generally have a clear vision by the nature of their association. Football teams want to win games. Manufacturing teams want to produce a product. Service teams want to serve their customers. You can lead these teams without an innovative vision because it is inherent in the structure, but the team will perform at a higher level as leaders are able to expand on the vision. For example,

- Many companies make food. The vision of food giant Kraft Foods is "Helping people around the world eat and live better."

- The world abounds with retailers. Sam Walton's vision for Walmart is "Saving people money so they can live better."

Individualized Teams and Vision

People who are drawn to individual pursuits need a compelling vision in order to join their "valuable time and talent" with others. They fight the tendency to see others as obstacles to their own success.

Consider the swimmer who would never allow someone else to swim in the same lane at the same time. That same swimmer would join a team if it meant access to better coaching, higher-level events, and a bigger platform to compete on. To make that commitment, the vision must be clear, compelling, and valuable to the people involved. The person who prefers to work as an individual wrestles with questions that reside on the surface of his or her emotions when it comes to working as a team:

- How is this better than working on my own?

- Is there a way to work by ourselves and then combine results at the end?

- Am I assured that the others are not going to slow me down?

A clear vision is necessary to overcome the obstacles that reside in these questions.

Intermittent Teams and Vision

In terms of vision, intermittent teams are similar to interdependent terms. The campaign or event has an inherent vision attached to it. People come together because they believe in the cause or share a common goal, but they lack the structure or resources on their own to pull it off. The team will commit to the venture even if the vision is not crystal clear, but they will perform at a higher level if the leaders can craft a clear, focused statement of the team's purpose.

Interrelated Teams and Vision

Interrelated teams are dependent upon a clear vision since the individual members operate sufficiently on their own. They are looking for a way to be more productive in a specific area of their operation. They could do it on their own in a limited capacity, but they recognize the potential of pooling resources and abilities. To risk their stake in the operation, however, they must believe there is a compelling reason to do so. Like the individualized team, their questions are close to the surface:

- How is this partnership better than working on my own?

- What will this do for me that I cannot do on my own?

- Can I trust the others involved to be as committed to this as I am?

- What safeguards are in place to protect the rest of my operation as I get involved in this venture?

Mutual Core Values

All teams also function best when they share common values. The presence of a team means there is work to be done and a challenge to be overcome. It requires effort, determination, and sacrifice. When teammates are putting in the same effort, working with the same determination, and making comparable sacrifices, unity of purpose is maintained. When there is a discrepancy in these values, internal conflicts arise and productivity diminishes. As with vision, different types of teams require different levels of clarity when it comes to their values.

Interdependent Teams and Values

Interdependent teams tend to communicate their values to one another regularly. Since most of their efforts require coordination and integration of everyone's contribution, communication happens all the time, even if it isn't formal and scheduled. One person will thank another when their efforts help move the project forward. One person will also criticize another when progress is interrupted. Obstacles to success will naturally come up at meetings. Things will be smoother if there is a clear statement of the organization's values, but the nature of the team will ensure that the values get passed on.

Individualized Teams and Values

By the nature of this team, each person holds his or her own set of values. It is difficult to establish a set of common values because each member operates as an individual. This is one of the reasons there is such a difference in productivity between members. One salesperson will outperform others on the sales force because she has a stronger work ethic or is more committed to networking. One runner on a track team wins more races than others because he is willing to work harder and watches videos to identify aspects of his technique that can be improved.

A team leader's job on an individualized team is to establish simple, minimum requirements that qualify a person to be on the team, and then to continually educate the team to accept the values of other team members while staying true to their personal approach.

Intermittent Teams and Values

Intermittent teams must by nature agree to common values for the duration of the project. Results must be accomplished quickly and with intensity. Election and fund-raising campaigns come and go quickly with competitive fervor. Event teams rise up with enthusiasm, plan with diligence, and rejoice over the success of the event in the span of few weeks. As a result, the members of these teams can have significant differences in their long-term values in life but will agree to the values that are strategic for the task at hand. Whether it is planned or not, the first thing this team does is agree on their values.

Let me illustrate from a singles event our team planned recently. We met six months prior to the event to get organized. At the initial meeting, the following questions came up:

- What is the goal of this event?

- How many people are we planning for?

- Who is our target market for this event?

- How are we are going to advertise?

- How much effort do we want to put into personal invitations?

- How will we maintain the quality of our printed materials?

These were all questions that forced us to talk about our values. It was interesting to notice that in the room were people who preferred to work independently, people who preferred to be on a team with long-term goals and routines, and people who loved the idea of a short-term project. The independent people argued over the values because they didn't want to feel handcuffed by restrictions. The short-termers loved the discussion and thought every decision was a good one. The inter-dependent folks waited patiently until the values were established and then enthusiastically committed to follow the plan. By the end of that first meeting, we agreed on the following values:

- We will pray ahead of time for everyone who comes to the event.

- We will ask God to have a bigger impact in people's lives than our plans could have on their own.

- We will seek for excellence in everything we do in this event. This means everything gets appropriate focus and attention based on its priority.

- We will commit ourselves to making a great first impression.

- We will work hard to get the word out to people in our network.

- We will plan every aspect of the event with professional singles in mind.

We also identified the following objectives for the event:

- Seek to get two hundred people to attend.
- Create a fifties' atmosphere.
- Celebrate the release of *The 10 Best Decisions a Single Can Make*.
- Include a signed book with each registration.
- Sell an additional twenty-five books to those in attendance (for siblings, friends).
- Make a great impression on the host church.
- Present a fun, energetic program.
- Get the email addresses of everyone who attends.

The whole process proceeded organically because everyone on the team had joined out of their interest in planning a Valentine's Day event for singles. It was easy to get people to talk about their expectations, and finding values we could agree on was relatively simple.

Interrelated Teams and Values

It is vital that interrelated teams identify their values because members of this kind of team have the most at stake. Each member of an alliance is an owner. He or she runs a business or an investment portfolio. Each is accountable for the operation of a venture. He is either rewarded by the success of his business or suffers the consequences if it underachieves. The alliance is being formed to enhance some aspect of a pursuit that is very personal to the people involved. Setting up the alliance requires trust, agreed upon goals, and confidence that the cooperative effort will be run at the same level as the business each member is running on their own. The core values of the cooperative effort is where I can test whether the rest of the team operates at the same level I do.

For this reason, it is imperative that leaders of interrelated teams spend time at the very beginning identifying their core values. If they don't, they will likely breed disappointments and conflicts over time.

A missions organization is a common interrelated team that many of us are familiar with. A typical missions group has a written doctrinal statement and a statement of their purpose. Churches who agree with these two statements are often willing to join with these organizations to support missionaries and send people on short-term mission projects.

Clear Operational Plans

In addition to agreed upon vision and value, teams are unified by a strategic operational plan that helps all the members know how to do their assignments.

Interdependent Teams and Operations

The operational plan for interdependent teams is a key determiner of their success. The primary question people on this team are asking is, "What is my role?" They joined the team because they wanted to be on it. They already agree with the goals and believe the leader has the vision and procedures that will lead to success. They walk in the door with the expectation that they will be given purposeful work with clear instructions and opportunities to grow. Once they learn how to do their jobs, they anticipate they will be able to repeat the tasks again and again.

As a result, those who lead interdependent teams do well to work hard at developing clear procedures and job descriptions. These teams function best with routines that are practiced and then put into action. Most corporations and team sports operate this way.

One of my sons was on a competitive cheerleading team in college. They spent hours practicing the same routine over and over. The performance lasted for about three minutes but the preparation time was about three hundred hours. Every member of the team had a specific job. Every move was synchronized. Every competitor was expected to do his job at the right time every time. If just one person failed to do his part, not only would the team lose, but someone could get hurt.

They put in the hours. They each learned their part. They challenged each other to believe they were the best and worked hard to be their best, as evidenced by the pep talk Zach, as the team captain, delivered prior to a national competition: "We've been training for a year to prove that we're the best. We are here to win. If you don't think you're the best in the country, you need to get off the team because we're planning on winning, and we need all of you to believe that."

It wasn't hard to create enthusiasm for the goal. It wasn't hard to say that they wanted to win. The key to their success, however, was the commitment they made to perfect their individual parts for the good of the team. The result was a national championship in co-ed competitive cheer.

Individualized Teams and Operations

Teams made up of individual performers do not rely much on group procedures. The processes that hold them together are simple and limited. About the only thing a swim team needs to know is when to show up and when the individual races will be. Independent sales people need to know how and when to turn in orders and reports. They don't need to time their activities with other workers. They don't have to work in concert with anyone else. They don't exercise moves that can either be enhanced or interrupted by the moves of the person next to them.

What's needed are people who take ownership of certain aspects of the organization and commit themselves to become the expert in that arena. Let me see if I can demonstrate with a small publishing and motivational speaking company I'm familiar with. They publish booklets and curriculum for work groups and lead corporate training seminars focused on interpersonal relationships and communication. In order for this business to succeed, they need creative development of concepts and products, graphic design and website development, office operations, bookkeeping, and volunteer coordination. The owner of the company is very talented in the creative development part. He works tirelessly at these pursuits and hands down assignments that help him reach his goals.

He has little patience for the other aspects of the business and gives them little attention. When confronted with quality control issues or financial challenges, he either gives quick, short directives or tells other people in the room to figure it out. Since he is the leader of the organization, everyone must adjust to his way of leading. Those who succeed around him have learned to take charge of some aspect of the company, set up their own procedures that are compatible with the way the owner likes to work, and then run his or her department independently.

People who love to work this way find this environment fulfilling, rewarding, and intellectually stimulating. Those who prefer to work on other styles of teams find this approach frustrating and limiting. It's not unusual for people to underachieve in this kind of environment if they don't prefer to work as individuals because it generally does not occur to leaders of an individualized team to explain to the rest of the team how to succeed. They assume everyone else will figure it out the same way they figured it out.

Intermittent Teams and Operations

Just like interdependent teams, the operations of intermittent teams need to be clear. Results must be accomplished quickly so the team cannot afford to spend much time designing the procedures that will achieve the desired outcome. The big difference in operational plans between intermittent teams and interdependent teams is in their complexity. Intermittent teams need simple, straightforward procedures. The team doesn't have excess time to learn complex, creative processes for solving challenges. They simply need a proven plan to implement.

Organizations that run a fund-raising campaign will often hire a consulting firm to help with this. The consulting group comes in with a proven, well-rehearsed program for raising money. They organize the team, train each person, lay out a time line, and build in accountability for each person's contribution. During the campaign, everyone knows what to do and when to do it.

Companies often run events as part of their marketing plan. They have a clear plan they follow for each event. They know they cannot reinvent procedures for every event, so they settle into a process they follow each and every time. In time, the process gets more and more efficient, and the team becomes more proficient in its implementation.

I recently had emcee duties at a fund-raising event for Alternative Women's Center in San Diego County. This is a yearly event to support the efforts of the center. From an impact perspective, it is different each time because they use different young ladies' stories and different keynote speakers. This year, a young lady shared the story of her son's birth despite advice she received from her parents and her boyfriend to have an abortion. Last year, a young lady told the story of how Tim and Pam Tebow's Super Bowl commercial got her attention and eventually led her to keep her baby. This year, Pam Tebow shared the inspiring story of the remarkable birth of her son Timmy despite difficult medical issues during her pregnancy. No one would have faulted her if she chose to end the pregnancy but we all marveled at the strong young man who now plays quarterback in the NFL. Each year people are inspired in unique ways.

From an operational point of view, however, the event is the same every time. For the past five years they have hosted the event on the same weekend, at the same location, utilized the same caterer, and followed the same schedule. The routine allows this intermittent team to get into gear quickly and operate efficiently.

The bottom line with intermittent teams and their operations is simplicity. Processes that are too complex or require too much innovation need too much planning time, which steals from the resources to implement the short-term plan.

Interrelated Teams and Operations

The operations necessary for a successful alliance are a mixture of the ingredients for success of the interdependent and intermittent teams. Since otherwise independent ventures are joining forces to gain something they all need, tightly monitored operational procedures are necessary to maintain trust. I will be willing to invest in the co-op if I trust how it is run today and have confidence it will be run similarly in the future. The procedures must, however, be easy to understand by all interested parties and simple to implement.

Your Team Experience

All of us, at some point in our lives, are part of a team. Making your team experience satisfying involves a few steps.

Identify your preferred style. Being involved with a team that matches who you are is one of the vital leadership decisions of your life. If you can identify your style and engage with a team that operates according to that style, you will raise your motivation level, sharpen your focus, increase your production, and intensify your sense of well-being. In other words, your life will be easier.

If you are attracted to *interdependent teams*, you will notice the following about you:

- Team sports are more interesting than individual sports.

- Corporations are more attractive than entrepreneurial pursuits.

- What you accomplish together is more important than what you accomplish on your own.

- You find security in the group.

- You like to brainstorm solutions rather than make the decision on your own.

- You have a need to trust others because you believe in group accomplishments.

If you are attracted to *individualized teams*, you will notice the following about you:

- Individual sports are more interesting than team sports.

- Freedom to work as you want is more attractive than corporate policies.

- What you accomplish on your own brings you great joy.

- Your personal goals are vital to you and they can feel threatened by the group.

- You like to make decisions without interference from others.

- You love to be an expert at something.

- You struggle with trusting people and get disappointed easily when others don't work as hard or as effectively as you do.

If you are attracted to *intermittent teams*, you will notice the following about you:

- You like to work with a team.

- You prefer short-term accomplishments over long-term processes.

- You get bored when the same project goes on for too long.

- You get a rush from quick results and the energy generated by events.

- You find it easy to trust others in the short-term.

If you are attracted to *interdependent teams*, you will notice the following about you:

- You like to work independently most of the time.

- You get frustrated when you can't accomplish some of your goals on your own.

- You like to network with people you consider your equals.

- You have strong opinions about how things ought to be done.

- You are willing to trust others but want to know that they will do things the way you would do them.

Look for work that is compatible with your preferred style. Once you've identified the type of team you like to be a part of, it makes sense to pursue career moves that allow you to operate in your style. We have only so much control over this process, so we need to be careful about being stubborn when it comes to accepting jobs. There may be seasons of your career where you need to work on a team you know is not your best fit because it's the work that's available. This doesn't mean, however, that you ever need to stop your search for a career that puts you on a team you love to be on.

Learn the skills that make the team you are on succeed. Every team functions best with certain skills. If you commit yourself to learn these skills, not only will you enjoy the experience more but the team will function better. The list below itemizes the "big-picture" skills that coincide with each type of team. You will need specific skills for whatever work you choose to do, but your ability to implement the "big-picture" skills will help set your attitude toward the work.

Interdependent Teams
- Maintain a routine schedule (arrive on time, work a regimented schedule).
- Accept your role because it helps the team succeed.
- Perform routine tasks with consistently high proficiency.

Individualized Teams
- Set and pursue your own goals.
- Work a flexible schedule that you set for yourself.
- Motivate yourself regularly.
- Determine to finish what you start.
- Define your work responsibilities based on the needs of the organization.

Intermittent Teams
- Maintain a short-term, focused schedule.
- Work intensely for a prescribed length of time.
- Flex to help other team members as deadlines approach.
- Maintain a positive attitude under intense deadlines.

Interrelated Teams
- Assess areas of strength with confidence.
- Define boundaries of authority with clarity.
- Delegate authority and responsibility without reservation.

Discovering the type of team you want to be on and orchestrating the members of the team to function effectively is hard work. It takes focused planning, robust communication, continual adjustments, and courageous evaluations to maintain your course. The results, however, can be stunning and often unexpected.

> A visually impaired man had been waiting a while at a busy road for someone to offer to guide him across, when he felt a tap on his shoulder.
>
> "Excuse me," said the tapper, "I'm blind—would you mind guiding me across the road?"
>
> The first blind man took the arm of the second blind man, and they both crossed the road.
>
> Apparently this is a true story. The first blind man was the jazz pianist George Shearing. He is quoted as saying after the event, "What could I do? I took him across and it was the biggest thrill of my life." [2]

Neither of these men believed they could accomplish the goal on their own. Somehow, when they became a team, their confidence level changed, obstacles evaporated, and they achieved what once seemed impossible.

The writer of Ecclesiastes understood the wisdom of teamwork nearly three millennia before:

> Two are better than one,
>   because they have a good return for their labor:
> If either of them falls down,
>   one can help the other up.
>
>   (Ecclesiastes 4:9)

CHAPTER 6

Decide to Major in Motivation

Motivating others may be the most important activity a leader ever engages in. People who are energized, confident, and eager to get into action are much easier to lead than people who are confused, bored, or frustrated. Motivating people is a complex system of inter-related influences, but some simple focal points can make us effective motivators. People do what they do for a reason, but the reasons form a short list. Four basic "whys" determine people's energy for any given pursuit and produce commitment.

Accomplishers

Some of the people you lead are motivated by getting things done. They tend to be focused on tasks and believe life is better when something is happening. They are deeply attached to their own ideas because they believe they are right. They are naturally confident and often pushy or demanding when deadlines get close. They love bumper stickers such as, "I am not bossy, I just have better ideas." They are also fond of such sayings as, "If I want your opinion, I will give it to you." They don't believe they need a lot of input or advice because they already know what they want to do and how it should be done. Even if they don't know, they trust their intuition and tenacity to forge a solution to just about anything they decide to work on.

When you communicate with Accomplishers, you need to be

concise and compelling. They already believe they are right, but they are not necessarily stubborn. If you present an idea that this person believes to be a better idea, they will quickly adopt it, put a plan together on the spot, and commit to the new direction. They just need to have a sense of ownership over the decision to change or they will find it hard to harness much enthusiasm.

Confronting an Accomplisher is often an event. They tend to be focused on ideas they have emotional ownership of, so asking them to change or criticizing any part of what they're doing can get personal in a hurry. They have already concluded that what they are doing is the best course of action, and they're committed to work hard to finish the project. Your well-meaning attempts to improve the part of the organization they are involved with are perceived as hostile takeovers rather than supportive teamwork.

Peter is a clear example of an Accomplisher. His approach to life was simple, and getting things done was often more important to him than getting things right. When Jesus recruited him, he did it in simple, straightforward terms: "Come, follow me," Jesus said, "and I will send you out to fish for people" (Matthew 4:19). He gave no long explanations, no list of reasons to convince him or multiple recruiting meetings. Jesus called him to action because he understood this was how Peter approached life.

When Jesus came near the disciples while walking on the water in the midst of a storm, Peter turned the situation into an opportunity. "Lord, if it's you," Peter replied, "tell me to come to you on the water" (Matthew 14:28). He didn't research the risk or call a meeting to evaluate the potential. He saw an opportunity and said, "Let's do this!"

Jesus's response is simple and contains no criticism: "Come" (14:29). If you're familiar with the story, you know that Peter eventually focused on the storm and had to be rescued by Jesus. But he was the only one who got out of the boat and he actually walked on the water. Even Jesus's rebuke, "Why did you doubt?" (14:31), was more of an appeal than a criticism. It's as if Jesus were saying, "Peter, you were doing it. You went beyond the others and experienced great power and accomplishment. All you had to do was keep your courageous focus. Next time, it will be different."

Consistent with his impetuous approach to life, Peter challenged the disciples to find a replacement for Judas. He probably should have waited for clear leading from the Holy Spirit since Jesus had told them, "Do not leave Jerusalem, but wait for the gift my Father promised" (Acts 1:4). Peter is a doer, however, so when he recalled Psalm 69:25, "May their place be deserted," and Psalm 109:8, "May another take his place of leadership," he enthusiastically applied them to the current situation. I'm not aware that Peter was ever criticized for this move, but it seems clear that Paul is God's choice as the twelfth apostle. We never hear any noteworthy accomplishment by Matthias while Paul is a major player in church history.

Ways to motivate an Accomplisher:
- Ask them to help make decisions for anything they are involved with.
- Put them in charge of teams, projects, or brainstorming sessions.
- Ask them to solve problems for the organization.
- Delegate projects, then let them figure out how to accomplish them.

Ways to frustrate an Accomplisher:
- Give directives with little room for innovation.
- Assign simple, repetitive tasks.
- Micromanage this person's work and correct them often.

Assistants

Assistants live by the question, "How can I help you accomplish what is important to you?" They are just as hard working as the Accomplishers, but they are more attached to your ideas than they are to their own. They show up wondering how they can make a difference by helping you accomplish what's on your heart. They tend to ask a lot of questions, but it's not because they question what you are doing. They are intensely interested in knowing what you want to get done and how you want it to be done. They don't want to make mistakes because they don't want to disappoint you or make life harder on you. So they often ask:

- How would you like this to be done?
- Can you tell me why you would like it to be done that way?
- What would you like to have done first?
- What are your priorities with this project?
- What is the big picture of what you are trying to accomplish?

It is vital with these folks to keep in mind that they are not challenging what you're doing. They are curious. They are fascinated with your plan and gain great satisfaction with helping you get it done. They want to know the plan because they want to help with the plan.

The beautiful thing about Assistants is their fierce loyalty. They are loyal when it is easy or difficult, convenient or awkward. They are even willing to stand with their leaders when public opinion criticizes them.

Matthew 26 introduces us to a follower of Jesus who was motivated by personally helping him. Jesus was near the end of his earthly ministry, and he was about to transition into the phase of his life when he would offer himself on the cross as the eternal sacrifice. His friends were unaware of the severe change about to take place, so they gave Jesus no special treatment. While Jesus and his friends shared a meal together in the home of Simon the Leper, "a woman came to him with an alabaster jar of very expensive perfume, which she poured on his head as he was reclining at the table" (v. 7). The disciples were not just unhappy with her, they were indignant. "Why this waste?" they asked. "This perfume could have been sold at a high price and the money given to the poor" (vv. 8-9).

But she was undeterred.

Jesus pointed out her value as an assistant when he told his followers, "She has done a beautiful thing to me. The poor you will always have with you, but you will not always have me. When she poured this perfume on my body, she did it to prepare me for burial. Truly I tell you, wherever this gospel is preached throughout the world, what she has done will also be told, in memory of her" (vv. 10-13).

Ways to motivate an Assistant:
- Describe the plan in as much detail as possible.
- Describe how this person can help in terms they understand.
- Compliment them often for how their contribution is moving the plan forward.
- Review often what you would like them to do. This gives them confidence they are doing what really helps.
- Make adjustments quickly when you realize they are off focus. They don't want to hear later that what they were doing was not helpful.
- Set priorities for them often. They want to do everything that will help you, and they can get overwhelmed with all that needs to be done.

Ways to frustrate an Assistant:
- Withhold information about what you are trying to accomplish.
- Ignore them. They will work alone very effectively for short periods, but since they are motivated by helping you, they want to connect often to ensure they are truly helping.
- Criticize them without giving steps to be more helpful.

Authenticators

Authenticators are some of the most valuable and most irritating people you will ever lead. These are analytical individuals who have a well-established value system, and they believe everything in life fits in their system. As a result, they tend to be black-and-white thinkers who are not open to shades of grey or negotiation. They believe they are right, and they usually have evidence to back up their position. They are adept at setting up and managing processes and procedures because they are fierce in their dedication to what they believe is right.

It is extremely important to recognize that their value system is just that—their value system. They don't necessarily do what is right, they do what they have decided is right according to their values. Once they have reached a conclusion, it is set in concrete and is very difficult to change. In fact, when you have to confront an inconsistency in the thinking of an Authenticator, you have to deliver your argument in concise terms, present it quickly, and then back away and give this person time to process it on his own. For the Authenticator to accept your input, he must evaluate it and decide to make it part of his value system. He will never accept what you say because you said it. He will accept it as "truth" only if he is able to create a place for it in his system.

The apostle Thomas is a clear example of an Authenticator. He had a rigid value system that he used to evaluate everything. Once he had reached a conclusion, he was absolutely sure it was the truth. Consider the scenario in John 11. Lazarus was living in Judea with his sisters Mary and Martha, and he had grown ill. The last time they were in Judea, Jesus's "Jewish opponents picked up stones to stone him" (John 10:31). This was evidently on the mind of the disciples because they said to him, "A short while ago the Jews there tried to stone you, and yet you are going back?" (John 11:8).

When they could not persuade Jesus to cancel his plans to go to his friend, Thomas worked through the implications in his mind and came to what he believed was a solid conclusion. "Let us also go, that we may die with him" (11:16). You have to love this guy. He did the math, counted the cost, and resolved to do what needed to be done, even though his conclusion failed to account for the sovereignty of God.

Jesus did not argue with Thomas, explain things to Thomas, or challenge his conclusion. Instead, he took Thomas with him so he could see the miracle. He knew that once Thomas was confronted with the evidence of Lazarus's healing and the protection God provided, he would adjust his value system.

We see the same approach by Thomas regarding the resurrection. "Thomas…was not with the disciples when Jesus came. So the other disciples told him, 'We have seen the Lord!'" (John 20:24-25). It wasn't enough for Thomas to hear the opinions of others, however. He needed something more concrete. In a strategic expression of compassion, Jesus appeared on another occasion and said to Thomas, "Put your finger here; see my hands. Reach out your hand and put it into my side. Stop doubting and believe" (20:27).

The strategy worked instantly as Thomas said to him, "My Lord and my God!" (20:28).

Before we are too hard on Thomas's rigid thinking, consider the interaction he had with the Savior in John 14. Jesus started the conversation, "And if I go and prepare a place for you, I will come back and take you to be with me that you also may be where I am. You know the way to the place where I am going" (14:3-4).

The words bothered Thomas because he didn't see the logic in them. This idea of a place Jesus was going and the disciples knowing the way to get there had not been previously discussed or explained. In response, Thomas blurted out, "Lord, we don't know where you are going, so how can we know the way?" (14:5). This set the stage for one of the best-known and important statements of Jesus: "I am the way and the truth and the life. No one comes to the Father except through me" (14:6).

Ways to motivate an Authenticator:
- Let them establish and run routine procedures.
- Make changes only when necessary.
- Choose areas of your organization in which you always accept their opinion.
- Leave them alone when they are focused.

Ways to frustrate an Authenticator:
- Try to be authoritative over them.
- Make changes that seem random to the Authenticator.
- Use emotional appeals rather than logic to influence their behavior.
- Force them to work with people who are spontaneous.

Alliance Makers

Alliance Makers love to be on teams. "We" is way more important to this person than "I." They love team goals, team decisions, team processes, and team accomplishments. This person's ambition is be a vital part of a team. As a result, they like coordinated efforts and consensus in decision making. They naturally believe that everyone has a piece of the puzzle, and when you combine the pieces, the result is greater than the sum of its parts. They gain satisfaction through the synergy developed when people work together in a common pursuit.

As a result, Alliance Makers enjoy meetings more than others in your sphere of influence. It isn't the meeting they like but the shared process of making decisions that draws them into the discussion. They want to know they have a strategic role to play. They want to know they can trust others on the team to be equally proficient with their responsibility. They aren't interested in doing other people's work because they thrive on the combined efforts of the team. They just want to know that everyone knows their responsibility.

Alliance Makers get confused when others cross lines of responsibility. They believe decisions made as a team are binding and that each person will carry out his or her responsibility with focus and dedication. When someone else does what was assigned to them, they feel as though the team is falling apart or doesn't exist at all, which causes them to grow restless.

Mary (Martha's sister) is a good example of an Alliance Maker. When Jesus arrived in Judea after Lazarus had died, Mary did not go out to greet him but remained at the house with a group of mourners. When Martha told her, "The Teacher is here and is asking for you," she got up quickly to go to Jesus (John 11:28-29). "When the Jews who had been with Mary in the house, comforting her, noticed how quickly she got up and went out, they followed her, supposing she was going to the tomb to mourn there" (11:31). She had an amazing ability to network with people and create a group experience, even when it came to grieving for her brother. I think one of the reasons she trusted Jesus so much was the way he responded to this trait of hers. "When Jesus saw her weeping, and the Jews who had come along with her also weeping, he was deeply moved in spirit and troubled" (11:33). He then went on to heal Lazarus, partly to encourage all of them. The result was a team celebration as "many of the Jews who had come to visit Mary, and had seen what Jesus did, believed in him" (11:45).

Ways to motivate an Alliance Maker:
- Create team positions.
- Assign clear responsibility to each team member.
- Help everyone see how their responsibilities fit together to accomplish the goal.
- Celebrate as a team when goals are achieved.

Ways to frustrate an Alliance Maker:
- Make unilateral decisions without consulting key team members.
- Do their job after it has been assigned.
- Isolate them from other team members.
- Ignore their ideas.

Experience Level

In addition to the motivations brought to the table by Accomplishers, Assistants, Authenticators, and Alliance Makers, people do what they do because of their level of experience. It's possible for someone to be proficient in one area while being inefficient in another. This often happens during times of transition. New skills, new technologies, and new procedures can seem like a foreign language to an otherwise effective individual. To keep people motivated in a world of constant change, we need to adjust to their experience level when we interact with them. Several levels of experience present themselves when it comes to the skills the people you lead possess.

Trainees

Brand-new skills mean that even basic tasks are unfamiliar, and the skill to pursue the task is almost nonexistent. The person at this skill level is dependent upon a leader to make progress. They don't know enough about the subject and lack the experience to brainstorm, trouble-shoot, innovate, or instruct anyone else. Instead, they need explicit instructions, clear guidance, and tight supervision. Because of their inexperience, you must be a directive decision maker. The clearer your instructions, the more motivated trainees will be.

When people are overwhelmed by their responsibilities, they grow introspective and unproductive. This easily happens when the skills they are required to apply aren't up to the challenge. To raise their confidence and help them grow, leaders need to take people at this stage by the hand and walk them step-by-step through the challenge. They will borrow your proficiency, your confidence, and your determination until they gain more experience.

The woman at the well in John 4 is a good example of how people who lack knowledge or experience are best handled with simple instructions.

- When a Samaritan woman came to draw water, Jesus said to her, "Will you give me a drink?" (4:7).

- "If you knew the gift of God and who it is that asks you for a drink, you would have asked him and he would have given you living water" (4:10).

- "Go, call your husband and come back" (4:16).

- "A time is coming and has now come when the true wor-shipers will worship the Father in the Spirit and in truth… God is spirit, and his worshipers must worship in the Spirit and in truth" (4:23-24).

- The woman said, "I know that Messiah" (called Christ) "is coming. When he comes, he will explain everything to us." Then Jesus declared, "I, the one speaking to you—I am he" (4:25-26).

When it comes to spiritual truth, this woman is a trainee. Jesus does not enter into complex discussions about the differences between the

Jews and the Samaritans. He doesn't ask her intricate questions about her history or her understanding of theology. He asks very simple questions and gives clear, direct, concise instructions.

You motivate people when their skills are in infancy by:
- assigning tasks
- giving clear instructions on how to do what you expect
- reviewing their work often
- providing course corrections often to raise their confidence that they are on track

You frustrate people when their skills are in infancy by:
- giving vague instructions
- expecting them to work independently
- asking them to solve problems in areas they don't understand
- using emotional appeals to work harder when they aren't sure what to do

Performers

As people practice their skills, they become more proficient. They move out of the infancy stage, but the skills are still a little awkward and inefficient. Their confidence level is growing, and they begin to become aware of the possibilities. They want to explore, try new responsibilities, seek out new ways of doing their job.

As a leader, they need you to direct them. You will be more aware of their limitations and abilities than they are at this point. The new skills are still unfamiliar to them, so they aren't sure what they are capable of and what they ought to avoid. They will also have the tendency to get overly enthusiastic about new experiences and spend too much time and effort in their pursuit. It's up to you to help them set boundaries, manage their time, focus their efforts, and rein in their enthusiasm.

Competitors

As skills continue to grow, confidence increases. At some point, the person decides they can do what is required. They start to take ownership of the process and begin to innovate how it is accomplished. At this point, they can become cocky and mildly resistant to instruction. As proficiency increases, so does self-evaluation. A new set of questions begins to surface in the heart of the individual. Am I a worker or a manager? Am I a leader or a follower? Am I more of a team player or do I like to work alone? If I could design the type of work I do, what would I be doing?

Just as teenagers move from peer group to peer group, experimenting with different identities, these workers try on different identities to see what fits them best. Prior to this stage of experience, the individual was not able to even ask these questions because they had to be so focused on learning the skills before them. Now that they can do their job, they have time and energy to think about who they are and what they want to do with their time.

As a leader, you want to turn into a coach at this point. The people you are leading are starting to become skilled and are able to innovate. It's now time for them to start problem solving and exploring ways of improving the work environment. You want to stop providing straightforward solutions since that will encourage the people you lead to backtrack in their maturity. It's more strategic to confront them with problems and decisions while you maintain veto power over the final direction. When you want to give instructions, try these approaches:

- What do you think we should do about this?

- What do you think is the best course of action?

- Can you put together a proposal for how we should approach this and present it to the team?

- If you were in my position, how would you handle this?

It will feel inefficient at first because you have more experience, more wisdom, and a busier schedule than the person you are training.

You will easily be tempted to skip this step in the development of those you lead. You'll conclude you don't have time for the process and you can get more done by simply giving out orders. If you give in to this temptation, however, your trainees will not develop under your leadership. They will forever need you to delineate their tasks, instruct them in their responsibilities, and provide tight controls. It will be like having a team of children around you who love being together while they underachieve.

If you fail to grasp this principle, you will continually be frustrated with people. You will say things like:

- "Why can't these people figure things out on their own?"
- "They've been here long enough. By now they should know how to do their job."
- "Why does everyone bring all their questions to me? Can't anyone else answer them?"
- "I have told them how to do this over and over. Why can't they get it?"
- "They showed so much promise at the beginning. I don't understand why they aren't progressing."

This principle needs to be balanced with the unique abilities of the people you lead because not everyone is capable of the same work. Some people fail to progress because they are in the wrong position. They hit a natural plateau, the limit of what they are capable of accomplishing. If, after an honest evaluation, you determine this person is misplaced, the best thing you can do for both of you is to free him from that responsibility. That may mean a shift within the organization to an assignment better suited to his skill set or it may mean releasing him. Sometimes you both experience frustration because God is trying to move this person to a new place. There are new goals to pursue and a new environment that needs this person's gifts. Holding on will only frustrate your efforts and prevent that other place from making progress.

Trainers

As people continue to grow, they reach a point of proficiency where they are good at what they do and are able to self-direct their efforts. They have learned from life experience and have reached conclusions about what they enjoy and don't enjoy. They have seen that some of their efforts produce consistent results while others produce little. At this point, they are ready to work independently, write their own goals, and seek help as needed. The primary need at this level of experience is for consultants who can help the independent worker with the nuances of innovation.

The key to motivating trainers is to wait to be asked. They are invaluable assets in your organization, and they will work best when they have freedom to make decisions and responsibility for self-evaluation. Checking in too often gives the impression you think this person is still too immature to be self-directed.

As Peter matured and gained more experience, he was entrusted with large responsibilities because he was willing to tackle challenges. Others might have spent too much time evaluating the possibilities or looking for enough support from others before they went into action. One of the most notable examples is found in Acts 2:14, where Peter preaches the very first sermon delivered by the newly born church. "Then Peter stood up with the Eleven, raised his voice and addressed the crowd: 'Fellow Jews and all of you who live in Jerusalem, let me explain this to you; listen carefully to what I say.'" And God's hand of favor was obviously applied to the message since "about three thousand were added to their number that day."

Coaches

A few people will stay with you long enough and become skilled enough that they are better than you at some aspects of the vision you're working toward. They grow to the point where they become true peers. They may become better managers, better at technology, better at coaching teams, or better problem solvers than you. At this point, you have the opportunity to pursue more sophisticated ventures because your talent pool expands dramatically. It's no longer all up to you. You have another peer leader on board who can guide and train people, find creative solutions to obstacles, and oversee entire areas of the operation. They can also add a higher level of achievement to their areas of expertise than you could because they possess superior talent there. If you can avoid jealousy and decide to trust each other, you can expand your influence exponentially.

John the Baptist is an example of how Jesus responds to a mature leader. John was a self-directed, capable, influential leader. He was revered by the people and respected by the leaders of his day. He was the one person on earth who was the closest to being a peer of Jesus. As a result, Jesus communicated with him differently than with others. When John resisted Jesus's request to be baptized, Jesus said to him, "Let it be so now; it is proper for us to do this to fulfill all righteousness" (Matthew 3:15). It was a unique request because no one else had a mature enough grasp on what God was doing to keep pace with Jesus.

Later, when John found himself isolated in prison, he wondered if the sacrifice and years of hard work had been worth it. He sent his followers to ask Jesus, "Are you the one who is to come, or should we expect someone else?" (Luke 7:20).

Jesus responded, "Go back and report to John what you have seen and heard: The blind receive sight, the lame walk, those who have leprosy are cleansed, the deaf hear, the dead are raised, and the good news is proclaimed to the poor. Blessed is anyone who does not stumble on account of me" (7:22-23).

John understood the vision and had an experienced grasp of the plan. He was discouraged by the difficulty of his circumstances, but once he heard Jesus refer back to the vision, it rejuvenated his hope.

As you consider your own motivation and ways to get the most out of the people you lead, place each of them on the chart below to identify ways to effectively lead them.

Why People Do What They Do

Experience level		Accomplisher	Assistant	Authenticator	Alliance Maker
	Trainee	Give clear, simple instructions. Provide consistent oversight.	Give clear, simple instructions. Provide consistent oversight.	Give clear, simple instructions. Provide consistent oversight.	Give clear, simple instructions. Provide consistent oversight.
	Performer	Communicate clear goals. Assign tasks that can be accomplished quickly. Look for assignments they have personal interest in.	Describe vision. Demonstrate how individual contributions help reach goals. Compliment often.	Written descriptions. Assign routine tasks. Give logical feedback.	Explain team goals. Demonstrate how individual efforts help the team.
	Competitor	Ask for input on goal-setting. Ask for input on evaluations. Ask what assignments they think they would do best.	Ask them how they think they can improve to help others grasp the vision. Ask them to help others understand their roles.	Ask for input on processes. Use short discussions to explain goals and priorities. Ask them to evaluate routine procedures.	Ask them to describe team goals. Ask them to show how their assignments coordinate with others.

Experience level				
Trainer	Set own goals. Use self-evaluations to review performance. Set own training program and schedule.	Ask them to help others grasp the vision. Ask them to help others understand their roles.	Let them choose routine procedures. Have them train others in routine procedures. Make changes only when necessary. Give concise, logical reasons for change.	Invite to strategic planning meetings. Seek consensus in decisions. Trust them to do their job. Allow them to decide how to train others.
Coach	Put in charge of own department. Have minimal and focused meetings. Let them decide how to do their job.	Assign a position that helps you significantly. Share often how their efforts help you be more effective. Have them represent you to others for orientation, training, and problem solving.	Put in charge of a department. Provide autonomy. Stick to agreed upon decisions. Prepare conversations ahead of time. Present your case quickly and logically.	Set goals together. Evaluate progress together. Celebrate accomplishments together.

CHAPTER 7

Decide to Be Relational

Bruce was a retired businessman who agreed to drive Pam and me from the conference center to the hotel room. He walked with a limp and didn't have much to say during the conference. He and his wife quickly volunteered to drive us, so I expected they would be nice people. But I never suspected his words would clarify for me a vital leadership principle.

Over lunch, Bruce told me, "The most important lesson I have learned in life is 'in the same way you judge others, you will be judged' [Matthew 7:2]. I grew up in a home of rejection. It was the one thing I could count on from my parents. I spent too much of my adult life judging that others would do the same thing. I judged my wife as some-one who would reject me, so I kept my distance emotionally. I judged people I did business with as people who would reject me, so I was either overly cautious with them or overeager to please them. Amazingly, they all seemed to reject me when I needed them the most. I ensured they would do the very thing I wanted them not to do."

My first thought when he finished was, *the judgments we put on people are like boomerangs that are guaranteed to come back to us.*

- The spouse who is consistently complaining about the immaturity of the other seems to constantly get immature reactions.

- The child who is consistently accused of being irresponsible frustrates her parents with ongoing irresponsibility.

- The friends who talk about how mean other people are seem to be surrounded by mean people.

- The leader who complains about the lack of initiative among the employees is perplexed that no one takes initiative.

- The individual who refuses to forgive can always find someone close by who is emotionally unhealthy.

- The person who is afraid of failure, rejection, or abandonment is usually in close contact with people who trigger the fear.

In a positive sense, however:

- The spouse who consistently compliments the other talks about marriage as one of the most valuable assets of life.

- The child who is consistently told, "I am confident you will make good decisions," tends to develop a healthy lifestyle.

- Friends who talk about how others have contributed to their lives tend to be surrounded by positive people.

- Leaders who include others in planning, evaluating, and decision making tend to develop highly productive environments.

A Long View of Life

Honest leaders accept that the journey is worth it even though people are a challenge to lead. Helping others is a roller coaster of victories and disappointments. It would not be difficult to become selfish and defensive in dealing with people if we take a short-term view of their potential.

Early in the book of Judges, the nation of Israel tested God's patience. "Then the Israelites did evil in the eyes of the LORD and served the Baals. They forsook the LORD…They followed and worshiped various gods of the peoples around them. They aroused the LORD's anger" (Judges 2:11-12). In an attempt to get their attention, "the LORD gave them into the hands of raiders who plundered them. He sold them into the hands of their enemies all around, whom they were no longer able to resist. Whenever Israel went out to fight, the hand of the LORD was against them to defeat them, just as he had sworn to them" (2:14-15).

It would be easy to conclude that the Israelites were not worth the effort. They were given the greatest privilege on earth. They knew God and had his personal protection, provision, and partnership. They were guaranteed success and security as they cooperated with him. Instead of embracing the privilege, they despised it and sabotaged it. They rejected the One who truly loved them and had worked tirelessly to give them a good life. They trivialized the commitment they had made to one another to become involved in silly, self-destructive behavior. Even when life became hard for them, they refused to return to their senses.

Perhaps you are starting to insert names from your own experience because this scenario has been written over and over throughout history. Spouses can be extremely difficult to love at times. Kids can be nearly impossible to raise. Friends can quickly change from comrades to competitors. People we work with can be stubborn and manipulative. It's easy to point out the flaws in others, but healthy relationships begin with us because our behavior acts as a magnet that, over time, determines the type of people who are drawn into our sphere of influence.

When the nation of Israel got to the point that they were in great distress, "then the LORD raised up judges" (2:15-16). He could have rejected them, but he raised up judges. He could have given up on them, but he raised up judges. Why would God continue to love and protect these people? It was for the harvest! God knew that the Savior of the world would be born in the nation of Israel. Today they were hard to love, but in due time they would become a blessing to the whole world, and God would eventually be surrounded by people he would call friends.

If I want to be surrounded by responsible, compassionate, forward-thinking, innovative people, I need to give others real responsibility and express confidence that they can live up to the challenge. If I want to associate with emotionally healthy individuals, I need to forgive whatever grievances I have against others (Colossians 3:13). If, for whatever reason, I prefer to attract negative, underachieving, critical people, I can choose to criticize them often and micromanage their work while I am unapproachable and demanding. The people I lead act like a mirror, helping me see my own approach to relationships.

It Starts at the Top

At the end of the day, life is about relationships. For this reason, leadership effectiveness is either energized or hindered by the way you handle your relationships. Jesus even defines eternal salvation in terms of relationships. "Now this is eternal life: that they know you, the only true God, and Jesus Christ, whom you have sent" (John 17:3). The greatest venture in history, orchestrated by the greatest being in the universe, is defined as a relationship with God and with his Son.

As was their practice, Jesus and his disciples got in a boat to cross the Sea of Galilee. The Savior took advantage of the opportunity to teach the disciples an extremely important lesson in life. "Be careful," he said to them. "Be on your guard against the yeast of the Pharisees and Sadducees" (Matthew 16:6). The yeast of these leaders was a subtle and futile attempt to be self-righteous. They developed an intricate system that appeared to be spiritual and disciplined, when, in fact, it was self-effort disguised as religious devotion.

In contrast, Jesus called people to an interactive, interdependent way of doing things: "I am the vine; you are the branches. If you remain in me and I in you, you will bear much fruit; apart from me you can do nothing" (John 15:5). When Jesus says "you can do nothing," he doesn't mean that we can't do anything at all. History has proven that human ingenuity and dedication is capable of remarkable innovations because we are all created in the image of God. But we can't accomplish anything of eternal value or produce lasting spiritual fruit apart from Christ.

Some aspects of leadership that add to any organization's ability to succeed are beyond the scope of human ingenuity. For a ministry, human effort is worthless when it comes to issues such as eternal salvation, standing justified before God, and accomplishing his will on earth. All ventures work better when the leaders involved are overcoming their sinful natures and finding the resources to live free from condemnation, and only grace and the indwelling presence of the Holy Spirit can address these needs.

Human effort can imitate these pursuits, but human effort lacks the redemptive power that turns the desire to be effective into character. We can appear to be religious, disciplined, sincere, and committed to righteous living without any help from God. It looks good for a while, but it is not sustainable. It's like driving a car with no engine. It will go downhill just fine, but then it must be pushed up the next hill before it can pick up momentum again. It's exhausting most of the time with moments of exhilaration mixed in.

When Jesus warned the disciples about the yeast of the Pharisees and Sadducees, they thought at first he was pointing out their mistake of not bringing bread for the trip. They fell right into the self-effort trap. Even though more than once Jesus had fed thousands with a couple of lunches, the disciples were locked into the mindset that it was up to them.

If we are honest, we are no better. When our schedules load up, we tend to think, *If I don't push myself harder than ever, this will never get done.* It would be awesome if instead our first thought was, *God is trusting me with a new level of partnership with him. He has big plans and he just invited me into one of his ideas. It should be interesting to see how he pulls the resources together to make this happen.*

Seek Contentment

Leaders who are content have better relationships because they are able to give more than they take. The more we progress, the harder it is to be content. We have better televisions, better phones, and better appliances than we have ever had. We have better modes of transportation than any generation before us. We have technological advantages that seemed like science fiction just a few years ago.

Just to give you one example, I was disappointed that I was going to miss one of my youngest son's college football games because I would be driving from Western Indiana to Louisville, Kentucky, at game time. But I have a cellular broadband card for my laptop. I was able to connect to the Internet, and I watched the game while Pam drove on the freeway at sixty-five miles per hour. It was awesome, but it created a whole new level of expectation. I now fight disappointment any time I miss a game because they are all available on the Internet.

The details have changed, but the struggle for contentment is nothing new. The book of Haggai begins with a similar scenario. The people of Israel had focused on pulling their lives together. They had built homes and businesses. They had their city functioning well and their needs were being addressed. Contentment, however, was elusive. "You have planted much, but harvested little. You eat, but never have enough. You drink, but never have your fill. You put on clothes, but are not warm. You earn wages, only to put them in a purse with holes in it" (1:6).

Israel could not find the contentment they were looking for because their priorities were out of focus. There was nothing wrong with their houses, their food, their clothes, or their professional pursuits. The problem was their relationship with God was being shortchanged. The temple, the house of God, was unusable because it was in shambles. "Is it a time for you yourselves to be living in your paneled houses, while this house remains a ruin?" (1:4). They couldn't find contentment because the issues of the heart were being ignored.

Every advancement is a potential distraction from the real source of life. It's easy to rely on social networking, virtual research, and computer-driven processes to meet the needs of our lives. While we enjoy these new technologies and rely on their abilities, we must not neglect the habits that put contentment in our heart.

Put personal devotions in your schedule. Pick a time and duration you know you can successfully commit to regularly. Then restart your commitment to this quiet time with God every day. If you miss a day, start over tomorrow.

Schedule focused times of prayer. During some of these times, bring your requests to God and talk over your responsibilities with your Creator. At other times, start with the simple statement, "God, you go first." Then, assume anything that comes to mind is something God wants you to talk to him about.

Create a routine of worship. Corporate worship reminds you that God is your leader and that he is worthy to be followed, admired, and trusted.

Take time for personal reflection. Life is more than accomplishment, but as a leader it's easy to get wrapped up in the need to constantly produce, perform, and push forward. These are all assets of leadership, but if they are not periodically interrupted, they raise stress in our lives to unhealthy levels.

God never told the Israelites to get rid of their houses or the advantages in their lives. He simply reminded them to do first things first, which is the secret to contentment.

Relationally Reliable

The most important leadership questions will be asked by your family. One man told me, "My eighteen-year-old daughter asked me, 'How can I tell if a young man I'm interested in is the man I ought to marry?' What would you tell her? Is there even an answer or am I just on my own to figure it out?"

After some careful thought, I pointed out that these types of decisions involve both objective and subjective factors. On the objective side, there are character issues to evaluate. I encouraged him to have his daughter make a list of the traits she was looking for in a man she would consider spending her life with. Numerous passages in the Bible discuss the importance of personal character. Ephesians 5 is one such passage that encourages each of us to pursue the following convictions:

Persistent love. "Walk in the ways of love, just as Christ loved us" (5:2). This is the kind of love that willingly sacrifices and looks out for the best interests of others. It is not, "I love because I want something from you." It is, "I love because that is who I am."

Moral excellence. "Among you there must not be even a hint of sexual immorality" (5:3). People who can be trusted for a lifetime have the powerful passions of their life under control. It is not that we want our desires numbed. We just want to have the forces of our life focused on healthy, encouraging, productive activities rather than selfish gratification.

Ethical encouragement. "Nor should there be obscenity, foolish talk or coarse joking, which are out of place, but rather thanksgiving" (5:4). The Holy Spirit who is in us has a positive attitude and looks for ways to build others up. Words are either powerful allies or destructive weapons, and we must each decide how we are going to use them.

Committed to truth. "For you were once darkness, but now you are light in the Lord. Live as children of light" (5:8). When we meet Jesus, we encounter the source of truth and are exposed to everything that is true about life. If we are going to be consistent in our relationship with him, we will seek to apply truth to our lives regularly.

This is a short list of the type of character God is trying to build in us. The list can certainly get so long that no one can ever measure up, but it is helpful to identify key character traits that make for healthy relationships. These types of questions keep us honest because we cannot demand from others what we are not expecting of ourselves.

It is remarkable to me how many times I hear, "There is a shortage of leaders today." With all the advancements in our society, all the educational progress, and all the training resources available, there should be a large pool of qualified, well-trained leaders ready to give guidance and energy to our organizations. Instead, the world is scrambling to find trustworthy individuals to be our leaders.

One of the primary reasons for this lack is that we have lost our moral credibility. People who can't keep their commitments at home want to be put in charge of productive environments. People who can't give credible answers to their kids want us to trust the answers they give in the workplace. People who fail to discipline their passions want us to pretend they can discipline the workflow in complex work environments.

The pursuit doesn't stop with the objective list, however. We all have subjective preferences that include personality, body type, sense of humor, sense of purpose, career pursuit, and social interest. I encourage young people to boldly identify these subjective preferences because they are a big part of what attracts us to other people. When the objective list and the subjective list converge in a relationship, we have strong confidence that a prospective mate has what it takes to build a life together.

Of course, there are no 100 percent guarantees in any relationship because we are frequently confronted with significant decisions that have the power to alter our lives. It is likely, however, that people of solid character who are attracted to each other for good reasons are going to decide to work through issues together rather than use them against each other.

Discernment Skills

The problem with the subjective side is you can get fooled. The emotions that rise and fall in relationships are powerful, but they aren't always smart. The history of mankind is decorated with stories of heartache, deceit, and disappointment because people didn't know the difference between temporary emotions and foundational traits. Three skills will help those who want to build discernment on the subjective side of relationships.

Listening

James 1:19 says, "My dear brothers and sisters, take note of this: Everyone should be quick to listen, slow to speak and slow to become angry." Patient listening gives others an opportunity to share who they are and gives you the opportunity to move beyond infatuation before you decide what type of relationship you are dealing with. Healthy listening involves:

- *Patient discovery.* Those who want to get to know others listen without interruption until they hear something that stands out. It may be a repeated statement, a statement that doesn't appear to fit with the rest of the conversation, or it may be a particularly emotional word. When you hear it, repeat it with a tone of voice that says, "That is interesting. I would like to hear more about that."

- *Persistent curiosity.* At some point, you will think you understand what the other person is trying to communicate. When you do, restate it in your own words, and then ask, "Is that what you were saying?"

Personal Boundaries

Human interaction and attraction are powerful. We have been made by our Creator to be connected to others, which creates powerful temptations. The only way to manage the attractions that naturally arise in human interaction is with healthy boundaries. A boundary is a decision that maintains respect by keeping the relationship in its proper place. God himself said, "It is not good for the man to be alone. I will make a helper suitable for him" (Genesis 2:18). Adam loved God and he was functioning at the fullness of his capabilities. He appeared to have everything he needed. But God knew there was a need in Adam's heart to be connected to another like himself. Graciously, God created Eve to be his companion.

It didn't take long, however, for things to get complicated. God told the two of them, "You are free to eat from any tree in the garden; but you must not eat from the tree of the knowledge of good and evil, for when you eat from it you will certainly die" (Genesis 2:16-17). In a world of abundant opportunity, they were told to avoid one thing—and they couldn't resist.

In general, they are both equally accountable, but the details of the story are fascinating. Eve was duped by Satan to eat from the one tree God wanted them to avoid. Her choice forced Adam to make a choice of his own. He would either set a boundary or he would ignore his resources and blindly jump in.

Ignoring the fact that we would all have done what Adam did, the best course of action would have been to take the situation to God. Adam and Eve were in the habit of having face-to-face meetings with their Creator. They could have easily gone to him, explained the situation, and asked, "What do we do now?" It's impossible to say exactly what would have happened, but it is certain that God would have had a solution that reflected his love, his grace, and his concern for those he created.

Ever since, we all have been in the habit of making rash, self-centered, short-sighted decisions based on our passions. Boundaries say, "I'm going to slow down here until my thoughts catch up with my emotions." Boundaries say, "I'm going to do what is right even if it doesn't feel like the best option." Boundaries say, "I will only take on my responsibility, love my spouse, accept my rewards, and honor my commitments." Boundaries say, "I will not sacrifice long-term integrity for short-term pleasure."

Practical Definitions

All healthy relationships are defined and behaviors are limited according to the type of relationship. Before entering personal conversations, engaging in physical contact, sharing social engagements, or making financial agreements, people interested in healthy relationships define the level of involvement. This is primarily an internal process. It would be awkward to ask everyone you know, "What type of relationship do we have here?"

You can, however, ask yourself this same question about everyone who is involved in your life. Those who determine their interactions based on the level of involvement tend to have strong friendships, productive work relationships, and intimate family relationships. Those who violate this principle tend to add complexity to their relationships and find it hard to sustain healthy relationships over time.

	Relationship Hierarchy		
Level of Involvement	**Type of Relationship**		
	Friendships	**Work Relationships**	**Romantic Interests**
Cautious	Acquaintances	Acquaintances	Acquaintances
Curious	Casual Friends	Colleagues	Casual Dating
Confident	Trusted Friends	Trainees	Exclusive Dating
Connected	Mentors	Mentors	Fiancé/Fiancée
Committed			Husband/Wife

The Hard Road of Compassion

Deliberate caution is necessary to determine when to hold back in relationships to avoid temptation, scandal, or deception. Likewise, courageous compassion is necessary to determine when to get involved in other people's misfortunes as an instrument of God's love.

Like many of you, I have attended remembrance services for the tragedy of 9/11. I had the privilege of hearing from Gregg Manning, a member of the New York Fire Department, as he recounted his experience on that fateful day and the weeks that followed. I don't normally cry in public meetings, but I couldn't help myself. There was so much sincere compassion in his voice when he described for us the six people from his current firehouse who perished when the Twin Towers collapsed. This rugged public servant then tenderly introduced us to his good friend, Dana, who rushed into the catastrophe to save lives only to end up sacrificing his own. Gregg was a living example of 2 Corinthians 1:3-4,7:

> Praise be to the God and Father of our Lord Jesus Christ,
> the Father of compassion and the God of all comfort, who
> comforts us in all our troubles, so that we can comfort

those in any trouble with the comfort we ourselves receive from God…And our hope for you is firm, because we know that just as you share in our sufferings, so also you share in our comfort.

Gregg was vulnerable enough to share his suffering. For weeks they engaged in rescue efforts in the rubble. The first body he encountered was a severed torso. He went to the scene hoping to find survivors but was relegated to discovering only bodies. Anytime they found a fallen comrade, they would call the engine company that person belonged to. They would place the remains in a coffin and drape an American flag over it. All work would then cease while the engine company silently marched their brother off the premises.

You could tell the pain was still acute even ten years later. A number of times he teared up and had to pause to recompose himself. The pain of his experience could have ruined him with bitterness, but it has miraculously been transformed into compassion. He selflessly flew to a little town in Arkansas early that morning to be with us. He came because, in his own words, "The whole country came to help us in our time of need. This is just one way I can give back."

We will all experience dark days. We will suffer the loss of loved ones and the loss of dreams. We will have financial setbacks and traumatic interruptions. People who appeared to be great friends will disappoint or betray us. Misunderstandings will arise with people who are indeed great friends. Those who dislike us will do all that is in their power to disrupt our lives. Once those experiences present themselves, we have a choice. We can focus on the injustice and develop callused, bitter hearts or we can forgive, seek the comfort God provides, and let it develop in us a heart of compassion.

Nothing is sweeter than the comfort brought by someone who has been there. They know what it's like. They know what needs to be said and not said. They know how to just be there and they know how to challenge us. When they say, "You will get through this," they are remarkably believable because they have already proven it is true.

When Shirley Van Epp says, "You will get through this," there is no denying her credibility. Shirley is the cross-country coach at Buckeye High School in Medina, Ohio, and she has had an intense battle with breast cancer. Despite a double mastectomy, a full hysterectomy, chemotherapy, radiation treatments, and numerous reconstruction surgeries, she never missed a meet and missed only one practice with her teams.

That is what love does. When it grips your heart, you always find a way to do what is best for the people you care about. You can imagine the inspiration her runners gained from her presence. In typical fashion, she claims to have gained more from being around the team than her runners gained from her. "To be around the energy and the excitement and the vibrancy of young people is just encouraging in and of itself. It's almost like they feed me life."

That was back in 2007. More recently, she donated her coaching stipend and engaged in aggressive fund-raising to help offset the $600 per runner participation fee that each of her athletes needed to pay for the privilege of being cross-country competitors. She doesn't look at it as a big thing because this is just what love does. [1]

Speak Their Language

I was walking to dinner at family camp when I got into a funny conversation with a four-year-old boy.

"What did you do today?" I asked.

"We saw crabs on the beach by the big rock."

"Wow, I bet that was fun."

"Yeah, some of them were dead and we saw crab legs."

"Crab legs, really?"

"Yeah, crabs need their legs to walk."

"Well, how does a crab walk?" I asked, hoping to get a funny demonstration.

"They walk like karate," he said.

I must have had a perplexed look on my face because his dad quickly explained to me that in his karate class they do crab walks as part of their warm-up routine. Dad understood immediately because he spoke the same language. I needed to have it explained to me in terms I could understand because I hadn't been exposed to their world.

God does the same thing for us. He lives in a world we have yet to experience and speaks a language we have yet to learn. He has initiated a relationship with us and has an adventurous plan for each of us to walk. He longs to communicate that plan to us, but he cannot do so in terms he understands but that are foreign to us. If he were to give us the whole plan, it would be overwhelming, but he wants us to be fully involved. He gives us action words, therefore, so we will know what to do even when we don't know the why. Notice in Psalm 34 all the action words given to describe our part:

- *Taste* and *see* that the LORD is good (v. 8).
- *Fear* the LORD, you his holy people (v. 9).
- *Seek* the LORD (v. 10).
- *Keep* your tongue from evil and your lips from *telling* lies (v. 13).
- *Turn* from evil and *do good* (v. 14).
- The righteous *cry out*, and the LORD hears them (v. 17).

As leaders, we will always be ahead of those we lead. We will have spent more time thinking about the plan, more hours agonizing over solutions, and more days dreaming of future decisions. Explaining the intricacies of the vision, goals, and future projections often slows down the progress of team members because they don't yet speak the language of leadership. What most of them need to know is the action steps that will help them succeed.

The Power of Personal Influence

We become like the people we spend time with. As a warning, the Bible states the principle as, "Do not be misled: 'Bad company corrupts good character'" (1 Corinthians 15:33). In an inspiring challenge, the Bible proclaims, "Remember your leaders, who spoke the word of God to you. Consider the outcome of their way of life and imitate their faith" (Hebrews 13:7). The influence of others is one of the major themes of the book of Judges.

Our relationships shape our spiritual convictions. "The Israelites lived among the Canaanites, Hittites, Amorites, Perizzites, Hivites and Jebusites. They took their daughters in marriage and gave their own daughters to their sons, and served their gods" (Judges 3:5-6). Israel chose to intermarry with these pagan nations, which led to disastrous idolatry.

It has long been known that men are greatly influenced by the women in their lives. Studies show that men tend to change their behavior when they are around women so that they become less combative, gentler in their conversation, and more careful about their attitudes and behaviors. Women, on the other hand, change very little in their ways of interacting and behaving when they are around males. [2] For the nation of Israel, this meant that the men shifted to the spiritual practices of their wives much more readily than the wives were won over to the husbands' beliefs.

Our relationships shape our morals. "The Israelites did evil in the eyes of the LORD; they forgot the LORD their God and served the Baals and the Asherahs" (3:7). The people of Israel didn't set out to make bad choices and make God angry. They didn't make it their goal to be rebellious or do evil. They simply failed to see the consequences of being intimate with people who didn't share their convictions.

We are on the earth to be an influence for good. If we want to maintain that influence, we need to choose as our closest allies those who share our moral convictions. It has always been my goal to be friends with people who disagree with me, but I am determined that my closest friends will hold tightly to the lifestyle choices I am committed to.

Our relationships shape our opportunities. "He raised up for them a deliverer, Othniel son of Kenaz, Caleb's younger brother, who saved them...So the land had peace for forty years" (3:9-11). The people did better simply because of the presence of Othniel. He was a godly leader. He had a clear vision of what the nation ought to do. He was solid in his convictions, steady in his morals, and sold out to the mission. The rest of the people gained confidence from him and discovered a new way of life.

The Power of Right Relationships

Our leadership effectiveness will always be tied to our relationships since we all become like the people we spend time with. That is why I decided early in my adult life to put Jesus on my list of role models. It seemed like a strange thought at first because he is so much better, smarter, and more powerful than I could ever hope to be, but he spent thirty-three years building real relationships. Jesus has authority as a leader partly because he strategically related to the most important aspects of life (Isaiah 11:2). As we follow his example, let's make it our goal to have:

Right relationships with decisions. "The Spirit of wisdom and of understanding [will rest on him]." I make so many decisions every day I take them for granted. I have choices about what I will wear, what I will eat, how I will organize my day, how I exercise, what my attitude will be from moment to moment, what step I will take in personal development, and so on. Each of these decisions goes much better if I have wisdom and understanding to know both what I should do and how I should do it.

Right relationships with others. "The Spirit of counsel and of might [will rest on him]." Every relationship on earth is flawed since it is the interaction of two imperfect people. Sometimes human relationships need a soft touch of grace, patience, and humility. People need time to grow and freedom to operate with their imperfections. At other times, relationships need leverage and confrontation. People can be stubborn, unwilling, or blind to what they are doing and need to be confronted with "might." It is not easy to figure out, but it makes all the difference when you get it right.

Right relationship with God. "The Spirit of the knowledge and fear of the LORD [will rest on him]." God is more than an idea, more than a religious notion, and more than a passive Creator. He is a living, thinking, feeling Person. To be sure, he far exceeds us in all categories, but he set up life so that we could interact with him. It takes knowledge to get it right since there is so much about God that we'll never figure out on our own. Because he is infinite, there is no end to his majesty, power, presence, wisdom, eternal nature, love, and more. Relating to him, therefore, always involves discovery and reverence. Amazingly, God created a way for us to be adopted family members and friends with him.

It is worth working on your relational skills because, as people observe the condition of your relationships, they will determine the level of influence they will allow you to have in their lives. You are the best leadership asset you possess!

CHAPTER 8

Decide to Identify the Influencers

Leadership was a mysterious concept for much of my early adult life. I was drawn to it, but I didn't understand it. Looking back, the subject began to take focus when I entered high school.

I wanted to play football but didn't know what position was the best fit. It was 1973 and the Miami Dolphins were dominating the NFL and Larry Csonka was the premiere fullback in the league. His punishing running style inspired something inside me that made me feel more courageous and tougher than I had ever imagined. Watching him cast off Pat Fischer from the Washington Redskins as if he were a rag doll pushed a button of motivation that started to move me from being a boy to a young man. When I joined the football team, therefore, I chose to wear Csonka's number (39) and went out for fullback and outside linebacker. [1]

After the first week, a few friends on the team approached me and said, "We want you to try out for quarterback."

"Cody's going to be fine," I said. "Besides, I'm a fullback."

For the first scrimmage, I was the starting outside linebacker but the second-string fullback. After the scrimmage, my friends approached me again. "Bill, please try out for quarterback. We think that's your position."

I realize now that it was a call to leadership, but I didn't understand it at the time. I just thought my friends were being nice to me and they were frustrated with Cody. They didn't have confidence in him, so they wanted someone to take his place. It was hard to hear the right message because I wanted to be the next Larry Csonka. I wanted to be a bruising, tough, hard-nosed runner. I didn't want to be a quarterback who avoided contact.

When the first few players asked me, I wasn't persuaded. I was glad to be asked, but their requests didn't move my heart to action. Then Don came and talked to me. Don was a soft-spoken, rugged young man. In my opinion, he was the best player on our team. When Don played well, we all played well. If Don ever got frustrated, the whole team was affected. The only reason I wasn't disappointed in being the second-string fullback was that Don was first string, and I could tell it would not be good for the team if he wasn't playing. When Don approached me and said, "I really think you ought to be quarterback. We could be pretty good together," something changed in me. I couldn't put it in words at the time, but I now understand Don was the key influencer on that team, so when he spoke, things happened.

With Don's encouragement, I decided to give quarterback a try and it felt right immediately. The skills required seemed natural. Running the offense seemed simple. Touching the ball on every play was very satisfying.

Listen to the Call

I was suddenly a leader. The team looked to me for direction. They counted on me to run the offense, call the right play, and make plays at strategic times. It was awesome and confusing. I had very little understanding of what made good leaders. I assumed that if I called the plays and performed my functions well, others would follow. I figured people would listen to me because I was the quarterback.

I had goals I couldn't quite accomplish. I noticed we had some talented players on offense, and so I set a goal of scoring thirty-five points a game. I didn't know how to communicate my goal to the team, however. I wrote it down in my notebook, but I had no idea how to export the goal to my teammates. We averaged over four hundred yards in offense per game, but we averaged only fourteen points.

During that sophomore season, I began to notice that a lot of the players rallied around Paul, a raw, aggressive, often immoral young man. He played linebacker and right guard. He was critical of many guys on the team and confronted others with apparent ease. He was also a talented player. I didn't understand it at the time, but, like Don the year before, he was the key influencer on the team. I was the quarterback and had responsibility to lead the team, but he was the one everyone looked to for confirmation. If I was going to reach the goals I carried in my heart, I would have to recruit Paul and elicit his support.

I didn't understand it at the time and didn't take any steps to recruit him to my goals. Instead, he and I argued for the better part of two years. He was critical of me and I was intimidated by him. Looking back, I realize he was trying to get me to notice his influence, and I needed his support but didn't have the skill to pull it off.

Raw Talent

Like Paul, many influencers start off with rough edges. They can be hard to identify as key influencers because they can be caustic until their maturity catches up with their impact. A college student was in a philosophy class that was discussing God's existence.

"Has anyone in this class heard God?" the professor asked.

Nobody spoke.

"Has anyone in this class touched God?"

Again, nobody spoke.

"Has anyone in this class seen God?"

When nobody spoke for the third time, he simply stated, "Then there is no God."

One student thought for a second, and then asked for permission to reply. Curious to hear this bold student's response, the professor granted it, and the student stood up and asked his classmates, "Has anyone in this class heard our professor's brain?"

Silence.

"Has anyone in this class touched our professor's brain?"

Absolute silence.

"Has anyone in this class seen our professor's brain?"

When nobody in the class dared to speak, the student concluded, "Then, according to our professor's logic, it must be true that our professor has no brain!"

For his logical presentation, the student received an A in the class. [2] His approach probably could have been smoother, but his influence was undeniable.

The Key to Making Things Happen

The first time I heard about key influencers, the situation with Paul made sense to me. He was instrumental in making things happen, and I lacked the experience to know what to do with him. I determined that would not be my story going forward. I would learn to identify the key influencers. I would learn to recognize that the people who intimidate me are often the very ones I need to recruit. I would learn to pass my goals through the most strategic people first so they could help me instill the goals in the hearts of others.

Key influencers are the people who really make things happen. They may have positions of influence or they may simply be attending, but they are the determiners of what will actually happen in situations where a decision must be made. If you are going to succeed as a leader, you need to identify who these people are and find a way to get them on board with what you want to accomplish.

The Babassu palm forest in Brazil is forever different today because an influencer stood up. Early in the 1980s, land disputes were settled with bulldozers, bullets, and brawn. If you could get to the jungle first, show up with a bigger tractor, or were willing to threaten others with a gun, you could secure land for whatever purpose you desired. The police regularly turned their heads and chose not to get involved. Diane from Christ's Church of the Valley in Royersford, Pennsylvania, describes how a key influencer by the name of Diocina put an end to this practice.

> These trees produce an oil that is used in cosmetics, lotions and soaps. It came from the leaves of the trees, so destruction of the forest was a death knell to those who farmed the jungle for the palm oil.

Workers in the field—all women—were unprotected, unrepresented. But one of them, Diocina Lopes, had enough. She was tired of sitting back and being run over, literally. She had kids to feed, and no other way to feed them than to harvest the palm leaves. So she rallied the other women and they stood in front of the bulldozer. And they did it again and again, until finally the government recognized their land rights, and shut down the practice of bulldozing for land rights. As a result, the women in this area of the Amazon jungle went on to produce a palm-oil soap that eventually grew into an export business. They called it the "women's soap"...

Diocina didn't have to step forward. She could have just moved on to the next palm-oil forest and continued to squeeze out a living. She chose to mobilize the women she had influence over, and made a difference in the life of that community. She and the women who joined her changed their future, and their children's future. [3]

I have learned that every organization or collection of people contains key influencers who determine the success or failure of any venture. Gain these people's support and you will be quite effective in your leadership goals. They will endorse your ideas, recruit favor from others in the group, and commit time and other resources to help move projects forward. Fail to include these people in the decision-making process and you will run into roadblocks at every turn. People who would otherwise be enthusiastic will be hesitant to get involved or resistant to the idea. You may ask them why, but the answers won't make a lot of sense to you because they don't know how to say, "I haven't seen Pete buy in to it, so I'm withholding my support." They may even believe it's a good idea, but they can't seem to find the will to commit.

Gain Their Favor

If you want to be a successful leader, you will need to develop the ability to identify and recruit these key influencers. Mel was one of those men in my life. He never earned a degree beyond high school.

He worked hard in blue-collar industries and never received any formal training in leadership. Early in his life, he was controlling, mean, and self-centered. He ordered his family around at home and was irritable with others at work. He often turned to alcohol to relieve stress, which made him even meaner and more unreasonable.

When his wife separated from him because of his behavior, he was stunned. Up until then, he had been able to intimidate everyone in his life. The realization that he was going to lose everything he cared about changed his heart. He gave his heart to Jesus and experienced a softening that he never knew was possible. A new love for his wife and family rose up inside. A softer tone characterized his voice. An unexplainable desire to serve others began to develop within, and a hunger for God's Word became his strongest appetite.

He started attending church and serving anywhere he could. He participated in any work day, served on committees, and attended any meeting that would help him grow in his new faith. When the church wanted to plant a new church in a neighboring community, he enthusiastically volunteered to be on the team. For years, he was the most faithful member of this congregation. Over time, he came to be recognized as the driving force of the church even though he never received a salary.

How Can You Identify These Key Influencers?

Influence in any organization is a force that develops organically. We see it every time there's a national election. A number of qualified, committed, and articulate candidates are presented as nominees. Through the process of campaigning, it becomes evident that one candidate is more influential than the others.

It is not so obvious in businesses, churches, or other community organizations. Through the regular course of activity, some people just seem to sway others. You can't simply assign levels of influence to people because it is not a position. Personality traits, posture, practical insight, and personal passion combine in a mysterious way to elevate one person's influence over another. Over time, people's ability to persuade others rises in some and diminishes in others. Since your ability to lead hinges on gaining the support of these persuasive people, how do you go about identifying who they are? Here are a few techniques you can employ to identify in your mind the key influencers.

The Look

You're in a meeting discussing future plans or seeking to solve some problem. Everyone in the room is sharing their ideas as part of an energetic brainstorming session. On the surface, it appears to be a room full of equals. However, over time, you begin to notice that with each new idea, people look over at Sharon. If she appears to be interested in the idea, the group explores that option with more focus and energy. If she appears to be disinterested, the group changes the subject and moves on to a new idea.

The look comes in various forms.

The most obvious, of course, is *the stare*. This is when people in the group turn their heads, focus on the key influencer, and wait for input before they say or do anything else. Less obvious is *the check-in*. This happens when people turn their heads to look at the most influential person in the room, but quickly look away and resume their previous activities. Even less obvious is *the glance*. This happens when the head moves only slightly, but the eyes move to see what the key person is doing. The most subtle form is *the blink*. This person is "looking with her ears," listening for how the key person responds. The eyes close to heighten the ability to hear, though not for too long to avoid becoming too obvious.

The Advance

Key influencers have a remarkable ability to create momentum. When they endorse an idea or get involved with a project, things start to happen.

I will never forget the day Mel convinced me of his dedication to the progress of our church. We had decided the nursery needed a facelift. Everything was safe, but the equipment was old, the colors were outdated, and the demands of modern parents were not being met. As part of the plan, we were going to replace the built-in cribs, which Mel had handmade. We had commissioned a professional cabinetmaker to build the new cribs with modern colors and an innovative design. We were excited to install the new equipment, but everyone wondered how Mel would respond when his handiwork was demolished in favor of someone else's giftedness.

The men gathered, drank coffee, and casually bantered back and forth on the fateful Saturday. You could tell that no one wanted to go first. Whenever we discussed the plan for the day, people would look to Mel to see how he was reacting. Mel picked up on everyone's hesitation and had a great opportunity to preserve his work. Instead, he got hold of a hammer, walked into the nursery, and started dismantling the cribs he had painstakingly installed years before.

It changed everything. All the men jumped into action. There was a buzz about the project because the light was green. The work was completed quickly because no one felt a need to cautiously preserve Mel's well-being. By the end of the day, the nursery had a wow factor that impressed young parents and gave them confidence in our ability to minister to the most precious members of their families.

This is the way it is when key influencers give their support. Hesitation disappears, plans get focused, and people's gifts go into action. Synergy develops that causes projects to move forward at a faster pace than originally anticipated.

The Wait

Once people know who the key influencers are, they will wait to take action until they know they have this influential person's approval.

We were in a meeting in Singapore, and the meeting planner was talking with the head of the maintenance crew. The planner was not happy with the way tables and chairs were set up, and he was trying to negotiate an adjustment. I could see the frustration rising as none of his suggestions were being taken seriously. Pam jumped into the conversation to offer a solution, but the maintenance man was not open to any suggestions. Although he was polite, he was stubbornly denying any and all requests. I started to get the sense that no key influencers were in the room, so I prayed for wisdom for a new way to approach this man who obviously took his responsibility seriously.

"Is there someone we should call if we want to make a change?" I asked as respectfully as I knew how.

"Oh, yes," he said. "Chen is the one who negotiates these arrangements. If he gives approval, it will be no problem."

In short order, we reached Chen on the phone, negotiated an acceptable arrangement, and implemented a new plan. In this case, the key influencer was not physically in the room, but his influence was definitely "in the room." Without his approval, all things waited.

Things to Keep in Mind

As you try to determine who the most persuasive people are in your sphere of leadership, there are a few thoughts to keep in mind.

Key influencers are not necessarily the loudest people in the room. Many people are verbal processors. They need to talk about their ideas to find clarity and reach decisions. They appear at first to be highly influential because they have an opinion about everything and the confidence to share it. Time will tell if they are outspoken because they are influential or if they are just outspoken.

Key influencers don't necessarily hold the top positions. The president of the board, the chairman of the committee, and the coordinator of the event may or may not be the ones who actually make things happen. Many people are motivated by titles, awards, and recognition. These people naturally gravitate toward positions that get them noticed, but it doesn't guarantee influence.

Key influencers are not necessarily the ones who talk with you most often. Influence is a God-given trait that can be humbly accepted and diligently developed but not manufactured. Identifying and accepting our places of influence is, therefore, a humble act of maturity. As a result, some people you lead want to have more influence than God created them for. Rick was one of these people in my life. He was a faithful, intelligent man who loved God's Word. He liked to get together with me to review sermons and evaluate decisions the church was making. His opinions were actually well thought out and intellectually sound, but people didn't naturally follow his lead. He grew to be a valuable sounding board even though he was not one of the key influencers in our organization.

Key influencers are not necessarily bold in personality or presentation. One of my biggest surprises in this area was Natalie. She was soft-spoken with a relaxed demeanor. She never demanded to be heard or pushed her way to the forefront. She seemed to never be in a hurry and consistently stopped to listen when people wanted to talk with her. She didn't volunteer for leadership positions and seemed to have little need to be recognized for what she was doing. But anytime we had an event, she brought the greatest number of people. People loved to be around her, and she had a remarkable track record of bringing people to be influenced by our ministry. We could plan a good event without Natalie, but we couldn't populate the event without her!

Key influencers have influence! You determine a key influencer not by the volume of their voice, hard work, dedication, loyalty, or maturity. You determine key influencers by their following.

How to Recruit Key Influencers

Once you have identified the influencers that make things happen, how do you go about recruiting them to help accomplish your goals?

Look for common ground. Your key influencers may be good friends or they may simply be people who care about the same organization or project you care about. You don't need to be natural friends, but you do need to find a way of relating to these individuals so you can develop mutual trust. Once you discover mutual ground, deliberately plan ways to interact over these issues. If you have an easy friendship, this is a simple process. You will both be drawn to the same activities and ways of lowering stress, and you will build memories you both treasure.

If you are not already friends with your key influencers, finding common ground becomes harder. You probably have divergent choices when it comes to free time and hobbies. However, you and they care about the same ministry, same cause, or same organization, so you share points of contact in common. It could be a training conference, a youth sports team, a building project, or an act of service. As you develop a relationship, you will come to appreciate your shared concerns, and opportunities will present themselves to make progress together.

A number of pastors served the same congregation during Mel's time there, and they all came to the same realization: if you get Mel to agree with what you want to do, most of the people in the church will also agree and get enthusiastically involved. Mel had an unfortunate habit that made it hard to recognize his influence, however. His personality and life experience led him to work from the negative to the positive. Anytime he heard a new idea, he would start to find all the reasons it could not work. He would point out obstacles, challenges to the budget, people who would be opposed to the plan, and various reasons why it was not a good idea. This was a real problem for me because I thrive on positive approaches. I like to believe we can and only give up that hope when something is proven not to be a good idea.

In addition, Mel grew up on a farm. I grew up in the city. Mel had a high school degree. I had a master's degree. Mel was more than twice my age when I became the pastor of the church he helped to start. We had very little in common at a superficial level, but I discovered we both think family is vital, the gospel of Jesus is the most important message on earth, and hard work is a virtue. I discovered we could build memories together by visiting at his kitchen table, sharing his wife's homemade pie. We found solidarity in praying for others to discover the truth about our Savior, and we built camaraderie through improvement projects at our church facility. Over time, we grew to highly value our friendship, which made decision making easier with each passing year.

Go to them first. The key influencers in your situation need to know that you respect them and recognize their value. They are invested in the pursuit and feel a deep sense of responsibility for the future of the group or project. Some of them handle this responsibility with enthusiasm and a good attitude. Others may be irritable or cantankerous under the weight of the mandate. Either way, they are your greatest asset. Before you go to the group with a new idea, new strategy, or any kind of reorganization, garner the support of the key influencers. It may seem like a hassle, but you don't ever want to surprise the key influencers with a new idea at a public meeting.

Ask them to evaluate your ideas. Your key influencers are the people who will convince others that your idea is a good one. If they have an opportunity to evaluate the idea ahead of time and provide feedback, and you incorporate their suggestions for improvement, they will be positive, enthusiastic, and persuasive. The implementation of the idea will be smooth and successful. If your key influencers start to evaluate the idea in a public meeting, it may still go well, but it will certainly take more time. These people will ask probing questions. If they like the responses you give, they will move toward a position of support. If they do not like the responses, they will hesitate, ask more questions, and may even pull their support, which will mean the functional end of this venture.

It didn't take long to notice that everyone wanted to know what Mel thought before they weighed in on decisions. I also began to notice that Mel was one of the biggest supporters of change when he was convinced it was a good idea. The point was clear. If Mel wasn't on board, the yacht wouldn't sail. If Mel was supportive of an idea, it picked up momentum quickly.

I developed the habit of talking to Mel before I talked with anyone else if I sensed the need for some kind of change. I would get together with him and lay out my idea. I assumed he would immediately start finding problems with the idea, and he never let me down. He was able to instinctively identify the financial challenges as well as the people who might be negatively affected. It would normally take about two weeks for him to look at the potential obstacles, find solutions, and convince himself it could be accomplished. Once he did so, he was the most committed, most supportive, and most persuasive member of the team. Since he possessed a lot of natural influence, his decision to be fully invested multiplied into unhindered investment on the part of others.

Address their concerns. Key influencers are vested stockholders in the outcome of everything that happens in your organization. They are neither neutral nor objective in their evaluations. They care deeply and are emotional about the decisions they are involved with. If they have concerns, they are intense and viewed as vital. You can't always agree with them, and they will periodically have a flawed perspective.

But if you have taken time to understand and address their concerns, they will be more likely to support you when it comes time for implementation. If you have failed to address their concerns, they will take the conversation public, and your chances of success will shrink.

Sincerely ask them to problem solve for you. Leaders are problem solvers. Groups need leaders because groups are collections of imperfect people and problems will arise. Some of these issues will be simple, and you will know exactly what to do to solve them. You won't need to give them much thought or deliberation. Other issues will be perplexing and will require research and collaboration. These are great opportunities to elicit the help of these important influencers in your life. If they are instrumental in devising a solution to a problem they care about, they will be tireless in their support of its implementation. It may take more time on the front end to gain their interest, let them do research, patiently listen to their ideas, and consider alternate plans, but the investment will be well worth it as progress picks up speed.

Mel and I agreed easily on matters of theology, facilities, and church government. One of the most sensitive issues we had to work through was music. We had succeeded in creating a multigenerational church, and it was awesome to have the energy of youth integrated with the wisdom of life experience. But it was contentious when it came to worship styles. Mel had an underlying fear that the older half of the congregation would become offended and leave the church. He didn't want to be stubborn about it because his convictions told him to respect the lead of the pastor and to trust God to reach across generations. The fear would, however, rise to the surface periodically, causing some very uncomfortable interactions. Out of fear, he would say things such as:

"This music is immature and irritating."

"We need to teach young people real music."

"We used to have musicians in the church. Now we just have amateurs beating on drums and twanging on guitars."

"Songs in church used to teach truth. Now we just repeat ourselves over and over."

Arguing with Mel was not going to make a difference, so I asked him to meet with me regularly for a few weeks to find a solution. He would make demands that we switch back to traditional music so we didn't lose people. I would ask him, "What do you want me to tell the people in our church who are asking me for more contemporary music in our services?"

Mel would blurt out, "We need to instruct young people to dress up more for church. They need to show God more respect." I would ask him, "How do we address the people who tell me they won't even come to church if they have to get dressed up? They find it easier to relate to God when they are more relaxed."

Mel would complain, "Too many people are standing through all the songs and being way too emotional. They don't need to raise their hands on every song." I would ask him, "What am I supposed to say to people who find it more satisfying when they are emotional in their worship of our God?"

Each and every time, Mel worked through the issues with me and arrived at solutions that enabled us to keep our intergenerational mix. We had some services that were very contemporary. We had other services that were more traditional. We created times when individuals in the second half of life could share their stories with those in the first half of life. We put more emphasis on small groups where people could build real relationships because we concluded we were less likely to argue if we liked one another. As I invited Mel into the problem-solving process, he became more agreeable and my respect for him grew. And, we got a lot more done!

Who are the key influencers in your chosen pursuit?

Choose one from the list and apply the following questions:

1. What can you do to build common ground with this person?

2. What problem are you facing that you can present to this person for assistance?

3. When can you get together with this person to discuss an upcoming decision?

Second Chronicles 10 presents a frustrating story of a king who refused to listen to his key influencer. King Rehoboam was the son of Solomon and the rightful heir to the throne. He had a great opportunity to unify the country and to create an environment of good will that would have guaranteed his success.

When the news was announced that Rehoboam was about to be crowned, Jeroboam paid him a visit. Jeroboam was a prominent man who understood the times they lived in. "Jeroboam was a man of standing, and when Solomon saw how well the young man did his work, he put him in charge of the whole labor force of the tribes of Joseph" (1 Kings 11:28). He understood the labor force, the history of how they had been treated, and the strategy that would gain their allegiance to Rehoboam. Solomon had overworked and overtaxed the people, but it was a new day with a new king. As an act of goodwill, Jeroboam proposed, "Lighten the harsh labor and the heavy yoke [your father] put on us, and we will serve you" (12:4). He had the ability to persuade a large portion of the nation to give their allegiance to the new king.

Rather than trust the influence of Jeroboam, Rehoboam decided to consult his advisors before responding. The king received two very different proposals. The elders confirmed Jeroboam's wisdom, "If today you will be a servant to these people and serve them and give them a favorable answer, they will always be your servants" (12:7). The young men who had grown up with Rehoboam said, "Tell them, 'My little finger is thicker than my father's waist. My father laid on you a heavy yoke; I will make it even heavier. My father scourged you with whips; I will scourge you with scorpions'" (12:10-11).

Something in the heart of Rehoboam led him to follow the younger men's advice while discounting his key influencer. The result was a great divide in the nation so "there was continual warfare between Rehoboam and Jeroboam" (2 Chronicles 12:15).

As a leader, God will faithfully bring key influencers into your life to help you move your cause forward. You will also encounter people with self-centered, short-sighted agendas. The outcome will be much better if you identify and listen to the key influencers.

CHAPTER 9

Decide to Rally to Risk

A heart surgeon took his car to his local garage for a regular service, where he usually exchanged a little friendly banter with the owner, a skilled but not especially wealthy mechanic.

"So tell me," says the mechanic, "I've been wondering about what we both do for a living, and how much more you get paid than me."

"Yes?" says the surgeon.

"Well look at this," says the mechanic, as he worked on a big complicated engine, "I check how it's running, open it up, fix the valves, and put it all back together so it works good as new. We basically do the same job don't we? And yet you are paid ten times what I am—how do you explain that?"

The surgeon thought for a moment, and smiling gently, replied, "Try it with the engine running."[1]

Risk Is Real

Risk is an inherent part of every leader's life. The very reason people look to leaders is that life is a risky pursuit. They look at financial needs and feel the potential for disaster. They are aware of relationship conflicts and are afraid to pursue excellence for fear they will be ridiculed or rejected. They become aware of the amount of hard work involved in a worthwhile pursuit and get intimidated rather than motivated.

Leaders don't help anyone by being foolhardy, but strategic risks taken at strategic times become the greatest moments in a leader's life. This was a foreign concept to me as a young adult. My dad was a very cautious person. Admirably, he worked as an engineer at the same company for thirty-five years. He lived in the same house, lived the same routine, stay married to the same woman, and weighed about the same his whole life. He helped put men on the moon while playing it safe in his personal life.

My mom was probably a risk-taker by nature, but through a series of abusive events in her childhood, she became afraid of people and of situations she couldn't control. She worked hard to isolate us from others, lectured us about the untrustworthiness of other people, and controlled as much of our schedule as she humanly could. Consequently, my mom did not have good instincts for risk-taking. She took risks that didn't make a lot of sense while avoiding ones that would have been strategic and influential.

As a result, my journey into leadership began with the need to learn how to take risks. Leaders evaluate risk and lead the charge into the ones that make sense. If a leader takes risks that are too small, the people around him will lose their inspiration. If the risk is too big, people will feel defeated. How does a leader figure out what risks are smart to pursue and which ones ought to be avoided?

Use a Long-Term Lens

Leaders look farther into the future than followers. Followers ask, "What will this do for me now?" Leaders ask, "How will this impact our lives ten, twenty, or thirty years from now?" We can't always predict exactly how our decisions will turn out, but leaders seek ways to reasonably make predictions. We study trends. We study history. We pay attention to life experience so we can predict with confidence how our decisions will improve life for ourselves and the people we care about.

The widow in Zarephath was at the end of her rope. By her own admission, she told the prophet Elijah, "I am gathering a few sticks to take home and make a meal for myself and my son, that we may eat it—and die" (1 Kings 17:12). Incredibly, Elijah asked her to take care of him first. "Don't be afraid. Go home and do as you have said. But first make a small loaf of bread for me from what you have and bring it to me, and then make something for yourself and your son" (17:13). She barely had enough to feed herself and her son, but the prophet asked her to take care of him first! And the reason he gave to motivate her to take this risk was, "The God of Israel, says: 'The jar of flour will not be used up and the jug of oil will not run dry until the day the LORD sends rain on the land'" (17:14). She had already given in to despair and planned her final meal, but based on God's promise to take care of her long-term, she took the risk, even though she must have wondered if it could really be true. She could easily have given in to the intense demands of her present condition, but the long-term lens of God's promises called her by faith to take a risk.

Looking back, I see that God faithfully led me through the training steps I needed. It started with getting married at twenty years old. It didn't make a lot of sense to me at the time. I didn't have a full-time job, and I owned only two pairs of pants (and one of them had a hole in the knee). I tried to convince God that getting married was not a good idea. The longer I tried to win God over to my side, the more miserable I became. So I decided to take the risk. I knew Pam and I would do well long-term because we highly valued loyalty and shared a common, intense desire for ministry. I just wasn't sure how we would make it in the short-term. I can now tell you that it was one of the most strategic moves I have made. God knew that Pam and I needed to develop together in order to fulfill the plan he had for us, and the best way to do this was to marry young and work on ourselves together.

Late in my twenties, I became a lead pastor for a church. I was inexperienced, idealistic, and intent on being successful. I knew that long-term success was dependent upon attracting a strong male contingent, so I began asking other pastors what it took to recruit and keep men involved. One of the recurring themes was "men go to churches that are building something. If you want to keep men involved in your church, make sure you consistently have some type of building project going."

Our budget was less than impressive, so the thought of adding any kind of a building project to our financial responsibilities could easily get me in trouble. I honestly believed, however, that men would step up and make sure we stayed afloat financially if they liked what we were doing. So, I lobbied the board to make projects a line item in our budget and strategically chose some kind of project each year to raise money toward. We remodeled the stage, remodeled the entry and lobby, built a playground, added walls to a large patio cover to create a new classroom, created an outdoor stage, and so on. It was a lot of work, but we never had a year where we failed to pay our bills, and we grew at least 20 percent in attendance every year that we engaged in a project that required the skills the men of our community possessed.

Plant What You Believe You Can Harvest

Leaders believe in harvesting. Seeds are small, dry, and often shriveled and do not appear to contain abundant potential. But when ground is prepared and seeds are properly planted, watered, and nurtured, a crop is produced that is exponentially greater than the seed itself. Leaders learn to recognize seeds and develop the skills that enable them to plant, water, and nurture seeds until they produce a harvest that benefits everyone involved. Every individual and organization has a number of talents. Some of these talents produce impressive results while others produce little or no measurable effect. When you think about taking risks, you want to choose the ones that will reasonably turn into a harvest.

James Dyson, inventor of the Dyson vacuum cleaner, stayed at the task because he believed his design would eventually hit it big.

> I spent about five or six years developing a completely different kind of vacuum cleaner. I built over 5,000 prototypes to get the system to work. Every year I was getting further and further into debt. In the end, I owed something

like $4 million. I took out two or three mortgages on my house. If I failed, everything I owned would've gone to the bank. Everybody thought I was completely mad. [As it turned out] I repaid the bank loan within about four or five months of first selling the product. The bank kept using me in their advertising as an example of how they loan money. [2]

On a personal level, Pam and I faced this type of decision early in our career. We had three children, I was in full swing as a pastor, and we were having trouble keeping up with our bills. We both agreed that Pam was going to have to do something to bring in an income. We spent weeks praying and probing for the right opportunity. We realized Pam could get a full-time job and do well at it because she has a strong work ethic. We were captivated, however, by the passion that Pam has always possessed to write. She wrote her first book at eight years old and, although it never was published, it grew out of the passion in her heart. I knew it would take time to develop her as a professional author and that we would probably have some lean years on the front end, but I honestly believed her writing had way more potential than any other career pursuit. Motivating her to write would take little effort. Convincing her to work hard at this pursuit would take less effort. The potential market for her work was larger than any other option we could think of.

We made the commitment that year to launch Pam as a professional writer. I'm not sure we actually made anything that first year. Pam was able to secure a couple of small projects and did freelance writing for a local newspaper, but expenses were equal to income. As a result, the first year was strenuous financially, but we believed we were planting for a harvest. The second year was a little better, but it still wasn't equal to what Pam would have made had she taken a full-time job. Going into the third year, we began to see the harvest. Now, twenty years later, it's obvious it was the right move as she has a full career speaking to women's groups and writing books, and we present as a couple at marriage and parenting conferences. If we had limited ourselves to just paying the bills that first year, we would have missed out on the harvest we both knew was potentially there for the taking.

On an organizational level, the same principle applies since organizations are collections of individuals. The organization possesses talents that work together to form some type of impact on the world. Certain activities have little to no impact. You can put almost unlimited energy and resources into these activities with very little return. Other activities are dramatic in their effect. The results you see have a synergistic quality to them, which means the results are larger than the time and resources you have invested.

For instance, I have noticed that when Pam and I speak together at a conference, the results go beyond the effort we put into the event. It is common for some well-meaning couple to tell us on the first day, "This is our last chance. We have divorce papers already filled out. If this weekend doesn't work, we will submit the paperwork on Monday." It is just as common for that same couple to say to us on the last day of the conference, "We're not sure what happened, but it looks like we may have found a new start. We found it in our hearts to forgive each other, and we're going home to keep working on our relationship. We think we're going to make it." We have checked in on most of these couples a year or more later, and the vast majority are still together and doing well.

We are not that good on our own. But God's hand of favor gets involved in this part of our professional life and creates bigger results than our individual talents warrant. Anytime we speak together, we expect this type of harvest. It makes sense for us, therefore, to be busy with speaking opportunities, and so we take the risk of keeping our schedule full with extensive travel.

On a lighter note, we have also noticed that, years later, people are still quoting principles we taught. We often get the opportunity to teach a follow-up conference two or three years after our initial conference with a group, so we get face-to-face feedback. It is not uncommon for us to hear, "I still say to my husband, 'Can you move from the box you're in to another?' or 'I need to noodle around a little, do you have time to listen?'" It's just as common to hear, "I still don't really understand my wife, but I do understand the way our relationship improves when I take time to really listen to her. I'm also glad that because we attended your conference, she now accepts my need to think about nothing. It was a real game changer for us." [3]

Again, I don't think these results are based solely on our talent. I have been preaching and teaching my whole life, and I have taught a plethora of great principles that no one remembers. It wasn't that these principles were less profound or valuable. It's simply that those principles are not where the harvest is in our ministry. It is one of the most humbling aspects of our professional lives. We can set goals, work hard, evaluate progress, and make adjustments in a pursuit of success. We cannot, however, determine which talents we are born with or which activities will be highly effective. If we want to take intelligent risks, we must respond to where we see the harvest.

Lean Toward Your Strengths

Leaders activate their strengths. Effective leaders recognize that their weaknesses are inefficient and time-consuming. Their strengths, however, are effective, efficient, and nimble in enabling them to adapt to the changing landscape of life. Leaders, therefore, spend time evaluating their strengths and the strengths of those they rely on. They seize upon opportunities that take advantage of these strengths and avoid circumstances that rely on their weaknesses.

Over time, you develop a track record of dependability and wisdom. With each decision and leadership venture, others gain insight into your talents and the way things happen when you lead. They discover the leadership activities you do well and learn to trust you in those areas. As a result, there are strategic moments when you must choose between competing and equally valuable pursuits. When these moments present themselves, you must ask some key questions that only you can answer.

- What is my unique contribution to the world? What am I able to do at a high level that is rare compared to the talents of others?

- Which of the options before me can I put my whole heart into for the longest period of time?

- When I look back at my life, which of these options will I have been most glad that I said yes to?

- Are there any of these options that only I can do?

I was faced with this decision in 2008. I was working in a satisfying staff position at a prominent church. I was also speaking periodically with Pam at conferences and writing books together on relationships. I assumed the two would be in balance for a long time, maybe even for the rest of our productive lives.

Then, both opportunities grew. The area I was in charge of at the church was expanding and requests for speaking were increasing at a rapid rate. It occurred to me that I could create a reputation for saying no to speaking requests if I turned down too many. I also realized the ministry at the church would lose momentum if I, or someone else, could not invest significantly more energy into the transition to a new phase of ministry.

It was quickly becoming impossible to do both. I was thrilled and disappointed all at the same time. It was a privilege to have two opportunities in front of me that would be personally fulfilling and filled with influence. I thoroughly enjoyed the people I worked with in both arenas. Both possibilities were loaded with potential, and they were both within my areas of ability. It was time for me to choose.

The first question I asked was, "What is my unique contribution to the world?" I loved working as a pastor, but I did not see it as unique since many people could do what I was doing. I even had the sense that others could do what I was doing better than I could. Speaking with Pam, however, was unique. I am the only husband she has. I am the only one who can be the "Bill" part of Bill and Pam Farrel. What Pam and I do together on stage is natural to us, and although it seems to me that many could do what we do, our specific ministry appears to be rare.

Others often say to us, "Not many couples speak together." "The way you two go back and forth when you speak is pretty amazing." "I hope you're planning to continue doing this because we all need it." In addition, I am fascinated with what I see happen during conferences and retreats. A lot of the preparation is done in local communities while a lot of harvesting is done at conferences and retreats. I am present at many decision points for people now, which is very exciting and rewarding.

As I considered the other questions, I had some interesting reactions. "Which of the options before me can I put my whole heart into for the longest period of time?" I could put my heart equally into either option, and I could have put my whole heart into doing both in a balanced approach. This question, therefore, made no difference.

The question, "When I look back at my life, which of these options will I have been most glad that I said yes to?" did make a difference. I asked a number of my pastor friends, "Could you regularly do public speaking together with your wife?" Almost all of them said, "No way." That convinced me even more that our speaking ministry is our unique ability. As I considered that, the thought that we potentially would not have maximized our ministry as a couple was unacceptable to me.

Trust Persistent Promptings

The longer you lead, the stronger your instincts become. Experience teaches you over time what will work and what will only create conflict or disappointment. We all have the tendency to come up with great ideas that don't stick. We consider them, share them with others, and then lose interest. These ideas ought to be welcomed because they increase our creativity, but they ought not to be acted upon.

Other ideas, however, persist. The more we think about them and discuss them with others, the stronger the prompting in our heart grows. Leaders take action when the stirring of their hearts remains consistent over a reasonable time period. It is part of living out Philippians 2:12-13, "Therefore, my dear friends, as you have always obeyed—not only in my presence, but now much more in my absence—continue to work out your salvation with fear and trembling, for it is God who works in you to will and to act in order to fulfill *his* good purpose."

In 1999 James Wood left a senior position at Microsoft during the height of the technology boom to start Room to Read, a charity focused on building schools and libraries in the developing world.

> During my travels, I met so many children in the poorest parts of the world lacking access to schools, books and libraries that I began cashing in small amounts of stock to help them. Two hundred shares of Microsoft stock was enough to build an entire school in rural Nepal. I eventually left my corporate job to follow my passion and literally bring books on the back of a yak to rural Himalayan villages. Eight years later, Room to Read has set up nearly 4,000 school libraries and put 3 million books into the hands of eager young readers. [4]

The congregation at our growing church was energetic and willing to consider various ways to help people in our community. They were an innovative, talented collection of individuals who put on school plays and holiday dramas every year. They were stuck in an inadequate building, however. The church property was located in a flood plain and was restricted by current regulations from adding any more square footage, which was desperately needed. The auditorium was full twice every Sunday, and the building was overworked with the active ministry and a growing school. Out of a desire to help families, the church ran a school for kindergarten through eighth grade, which kept the building busy Monday through Friday. The auditorium space was needed for classrooms, so every Friday the facility was rearranged for church and every Sunday night it was rearranged again for school.

At first, the variety of ministries and number of people influenced was fun and exciting. After a while, however, the strain on the building put a strain on the people. The members of the board realized that something needed to be done, so it became the topic of many planning meetings. Various members of the board represented the sentiments of different segments of the congregation:

"We cannot keep stressing the building like this. We're going to wear it out and it will get ugly."

"We don't have the budget to get a new building. We will lose a lot of people if we spend that kind of money."

"We can sell the property. It's in a great location so we should get a good price for it."

"We are in the flood plain. We can't possibly sell the property for what it's worth or what we need."

"The people love this building and the property. I know this is a challenge, but the people will figure out how to make this work."

For weeks we wrestled with the best way to handle our building problems. As the lead pastor, I could tell that somebody's opinion needed to win out. The other members of the board were attached to various parts of the congregation and had different priorities, so it became clear that we were not going to reach an easy consensus.

I spent a lot of time in prayer over this decision. I knew that if we moved to a different location, many people would be upset. They had invested in this building and they loved going to church there. It felt like a second home to many of them, so I knew they would grieve a move. I also knew many people would love the idea of a move as it increased our potential for influence and further innovation. There was no accurate way to measure the consequences of a move or the limits that would be imposed if we stayed. In the end, it became a judgment call based on an assessment of risk. Every time I considered the move, I had a strong sense in my heart God was leading this way.

"I think it's time to move," I said at the next meeting. "I don't believe we are in a position to buy a building, but I know that the elementary school auditorium down the street is available to rent. It's twice as big as what we have here, and we can have access to enough classrooms to run our children's ministry. I think we should commit to a rental agreement and pull the resources together to run a mobile church so we can keep growing."

I got the expected responses.

"I think that's a great idea. Let's do it."

"You want to be a mobile church? People aren't going to do that."

"I don't think people will give for that."

"People will love it. It will be exciting, challenging, and a whole lot of fun."

After giving everyone an opportunity to air their thoughts, I said to the board, "It seems to me we can talk about this forever. We are eventually going to have to settle on somebody's opinion. Since you have made me the lead pastor of the church, I think we should go with mine. Let's rent a new auditorium and challenge the church to reach this community."

Now, I am a team player by nature. I like an environment where there are agreed upon goals and clearly defined areas of responsibility. I also prefer decisions based on solid consensus. I believe people work harder and focus more diligently when they have ownership of decisions. I could tell, however, that we were not going to reach consensus through normal discussion. Everyone in the room had an opinion based on personal needs and reactions. The reasons for either staying put or moving seemed rock solid to everyone, and our interaction did nothing to change anyone's mind.

I finally realized that someone in the room was going to have to take a more decisive leadership role or nothing was going to happen. We would be stalemated in a nongrowth situation that would make us feel secure but would prove to be unhealthy for our congregation in the long run. I had spent years developing a team environment, so I knew it would cost me leadership capital to take this stand. I had to consider the cost ahead of time. If the group agreed, it would be capital well spent and my leadership influence would grow. If the group disagreed, it could be the beginning of the end of my ability to lead in this location.

I determined in my heart that this move needed to happen because growth is a biblical mandate. We can't make congregations grow, but we can certainly create an environment where growth is to be expected. I honestly believed the church would pick up momentum and increase its influence in the community if we moved. I also firmly believed the church would lose its momentum if it stayed put. Therefore, I was willing to walk away from this position if the other leaders were unwilling to do what I believed was necessary.

The room grew silent. The other men in the room looked at me and then looked around at each other. We all recognized this as one those moments that changes everything. It was either going to be a brilliant step of leadership or a great setback. As with most leadership decisions, you can't know for sure ahead of time which it will be. If it were always obvious, we wouldn't need leaders!

After a few minutes, the key influencer in the room said, "Okay. We hired Bill because we believed he was God's man for this position. If that is his opinion and we have no biblical reason not to do it, I think we should trust his instincts." And that is all it took. Consensus was reached instantly and plans were put in place.

It was awesome to watch people go into action as we shared with the congregation what we were going to do. A small group of men approached us and asked if they could build a portable sound system. Another group volunteered to research seating options. The worship team immediately started strategizing the best way to set up each Sunday. The children's ministry team put together a plan and presented it to the board for review before we could even request it. No one needed to be pushed or prodded. The reaction of the congregation gave us all confidence that we had indeed made the right decision.

Risk Creates the Best Stories

Risk usually seems strange at the time, but it creates stories you tell for the rest of your life. Just ask Peter, who was confronted by Jesus one day as he came home from work:

When Peter came into the house, Jesus was the first to speak.
"What do you think, Simon?" he asked. "From whom do
the kings of the earth collect duty and taxes—from their
own children or from others?"

"From others," Peter answered.

"Then the children are exempt," Jesus said to him. "But so
that we may not cause offense, go to the lake and throw
out your line. Take the first fish you catch; open its mouth
and you will find a four-drachma coin. Take it and give it
to them for my tax and yours" (Matthew 17:25-27).

You can bet that Peter spent the rest of his life telling people about
the time he paid his taxes out of the mouth of a fish. You may not tell
fish stories, but when you take smart risks in life, they will become the
stories you tell for the rest of your days.

CHAPTER 10

Decide to Seek Supernatural Support

God created you to be a leader. He knows how you are wired, what you love, what frustrates you, and the vision he has placed in your soul. He also knows everyone around you and how they can contribute to the vision. Learning to listen to the Holy Spirit in the midst of leading is one of the quickest ways to rally people to the cause.

The great need of leaders is voiced by James: "If any of you lacks wisdom, you should ask God who gives generously to all without finding fault, and it will be given to you" (James 1:5). It is a simple directive that makes it clear God is interested in an interactive journey with anyone willing to take advantage of the privilege. It appears God delights in doing this. "Generously" means he gives more than enough for the task at hand. "Without finding fault" means he never rolls his eyes or says, "I gave you wisdom last time and you didn't do anything with it. Why should I keep doing this?" Instead, he simply says yes when we are willing to ask for wisdom.

If you are willing, you can take advantage of the supernatural insight, endurance, and character God is willing to share with each of us. We can home in on the way God thinks about decisions because "we have the mind of Christ" (1 Corinthians 2:16). We can approach decisions with a calm sense of contentment as the apostle Paul demonstrated for us, "I can do all this through him who gives me strength" (Philippians

4:13). We can develop habits that keep us focused on the vision God has placed in our hearts because "the fruit of the Spirit is...self-control" (Galatians 5:22,23). In addition, we can discern the nuances of God's will for our lives and the organizations we lead because God has promised, "I will instruct you and teach you in the way you should go; I will counsel you with my loving eye on you" (Psalm 32:8).

How does a leader tap into the insight, strength, and resources available through an interactive relationship with God?

God's Help in Leadership: Walking in the Power of the Holy Spirit

A number of strategic skills give you access to the resources of the Holy Spirit in the midst of your everyday life. I was introduced to the skill of "spiritual breathing" when I was a college student involved with Campus Crusade for Christ (now called Cru).[1] Bill Bright, the founder of that organization, taught that spiritual impurities must be exhaled and spiritual nutrients must be inhaled in order to have a healthy spiritual life.

The spiritual impurities are what the Bible calls sin, which is any act of self-will that diverts us from accomplishing God's will. When we become aware of these acts of self-will, the Bible tells us to "exhale" by "confessing our sins" (1 John 1:9). As we journey through our lives, the Holy Spirit will point these sins out to us. He is so interested in us experiencing his strength in our lives that he stirs us up when something is holding us back. The Holy Spirit will use various means, but he will make us aware of the specific thoughts, attitudes, and actions that prevent us from being filled with his power. The purpose of disturbing us, however, is not to make us feel guilty. It is to get us to confess. Confession has three simple steps:

First, admit what you did to God. Don't explain it or justify it. Simply admit that your thought, action, or attitude was contrary to God's will.

Second, agree that what you did was wrong. Romans 3:23 is very clear when it comes to admitting our shortcomings: "All have sinned and fall short of the glory of God." When you admit what you did was wrong, you guide your heart to be cooperative with God.

Third, apologize to your Savior. The first step to real change is a contrite heart. If you admit to something but are not sorry for it, you are not really confessing. You might be sorry that you got caught, but that is a far cry from repentance, which would include being sorry you made the wrong decision in the first place. If you are not sorry or do not apologize, then you are hardening your heart toward this action or attitude, which will all but guarantee that you will do it again and again.

Once you have exhaled, it is time to inhale. Dr. Bright explained that we inhale by appropriating the power of the Holy Spirit into our lives. In Ephesians 5:18, we are commanded to be filled with the Holy Spirit. Being filled is different from being indwelt. The Holy Spirit lives in every believer, but not every believer is yielded to his guidance.

This is a dynamic process. Every decision affects who is in charge of our lives. It is similar to driving a car. Every time you get in a car, you have to decide who will drive. In the same way, you have been given the privilege of deciding who is "driving your life" each and every day. You can be in charge and rely on *your* wisdom, skills, insight, and experience. Or you can put the Holy Spirit in charge and make *God's* wisdom, skills, power, and guidance active in your experience.

Like breathing, we must do this daily. The process of inhaling is based on a simple, biblical concept. God wants us to say yes to his will, and it is his will for you to be filled with the Holy Spirit.

First John 5:14-15 profoundly says that God will say yes to his will. Ephesians 5:18 makes it clear that it is God's will for us to be filled with the Spirit. Notice the parallel here between the influence of alcohol and the influence of the Holy Spirit. I believe the parallels are linked to three ideas. Alcohol will cause you to do things you wouldn't normally do, say things you wouldn't normally say, and give you boldness not normally characteristic of you. In the same way, the Holy Spirit will help you say things and do things that are highly strategic, and you will have boldness to love, serve, and lead those God puts in your charge.

It follows, then, that if we ask God to fill us with his Spirit, he will say yes. This is inhaling. The only thing that can prevent the Holy Spirit from being in charge at this point is our sin. When we become aware of any sin in our life, we can confess it and set up our heart to be empowered by the Spirit once again. This is exhaling.

When we consistently exhale and inhale, we will become comfortable with the Spirit in the driver's seat, and we will grow increasingly dissatisfied when we take the wheel. Life is so much better, stronger, and sweeter when God is in control.

Practice the Presence
Each day this week:

- Ask God, "Is there anything I need to confess to you today?"
- Confess anything that comes to mind.
- After you have confessed, ask God to fill (empower) you with his Spirit.
- At the end of your day, write down the ways you noticed that God worked in your life.

Cooperating with the Holy Spirit
Following the Spirit's lead involves planning and adjusting because there is nothing passive about following. We encounter an active partnership between people and God in Proverbs 16:

> To humans belong the plans of the heart,
>   but from the Lord comes the proper answer of the
>   tongue...
> When the Lord takes pleasure in anyone's way,
>   he causes their enemies to make peace with them...
> In their hearts humans plan their course,
>   but the Lord establishes their steps.
>   (Proverbs 16:1,7,9)

We are challenged to plan our ways with our hearts fully invested in what we want to do. God wants us to search our hearts for the activities, decisions, and pursuits that matter to us. At the same time, "the Lord establishes [our] steps." God did not motivate you with talent and desires only to leave you to your limited perspective. God actively watches over your life and prompts you to make adjustments to your plans as necessary. In other words, he coaches us up.

The Holy Spirit knows just what adjustments need to be made, and he will reveal them to you when the time is right. And because the Spirit is God, the Creator, his ideas will be more creative than what you might come up with on your own. Your job is to make plans, get in motion, and be willing to adjust.

In addition to getting into motion, we need to plan with an attitude of prayer if we want to cooperate with the Spirit. We need to invite God to our planning meetings. Committing our way and trusting in the Lord means we have asked God for wisdom in our planning, guided by the following questions:

- Are my plans based on what I know about God?
- Is this something that God would reasonably be in favor of?
- Would I be glad to meet God face-to-face while I'm doing what I'm about to do?
- Can I enthusiastically ask God to make this happen?

When you can sincerely say yes to these questions, God gives you the green light and will get actively involved to accomplish his will in your life. When these questions bother you, it's time to slow down and take your decision back to the drawing board.

"Take delight in the LORD, and he will give you the desires of your heart" (Psalm 37:4). This is where following the Spirit's lead becomes highly relational. Many tasks need to be accomplished in life, but leadership is more than just getting things done. Leading people also includes motivating others, helping them believe in something worth a sacrifice, valuing relationships, working together to fulfill a dream, and sacrificing for the sake of the team. It can get quite complex when you're trying to sort through varying agendas, manage relationships, and train others, and we can use all the help we can get.

When we take our plans to God with the attitude that he is more important than our plans, new possibilities open up for us. God begins to open our heart to the dreams he has for us. Since his perspective is much larger than ours, he sees opportunities that would never occur to us. We will never discover them on our own, and when we are first exposed to them, they will seem uncomfortable or even impossible, but they end up being some of our greatest memories. The key is to make plans, but don't get stubborn. Keep your heart open to adjusting when the Spirit makes it clear that a change of course is best.

I Didn't See That Coming

"We should create a video studio. We have the room and I think we have the ability." I can hear those words spoken by one of our assistants as if it were yesterday. My first thought was, *That's crazy. Studios are expensive. Video production is time consuming, and we're already busy. Besides, I don't know anything about the intricacies of video production.* It was an idea that seemed unreasonable at the time, and yet I reluctantly had a sense that God was leading.

I tried to ignore it for a while, but the thought wouldn't go away. Over time, I could tell that I was going to be haunted by the idea until I did something about it. I borrowed money for lighting and got to work installing a studio where we could produce small-group curriculum to help people learn the skills we believe everyone ought to know. Now that we're committed to the process and have started creating curriculum, I can see the wisdom in it.

- I believe in small groups. I have been convinced for a long time that more growth happens in people's lives when they meet and discuss what they are learning than in any other setting.

- I love to teach God's Word and the principles that help people grow.

- Our assistant and her husband have experience in video production.

- We have plenty of books to work with as content.

- We have the space to house the studio.

Practice the Presence

Practice cooperating with the Spirit this week by processing a decision you are facing with these questions that we discussed a moment ago:

- Are my plans based on what I know about God?

- Is this something that God would reasonably be in favor of?

- Would I be glad to meet God face-to-face while I'm doing what I'm about to do?

- Can I enthusiastically ask God to make this happen?

As you discover yes answers to these questions, commit wholeheartedly to your plans. If you sense a no, adjust your plans and consider another course of action.

Worship Tunes You In

> You, God, are awesome in your sanctuary;
>> the God of Israel gives power and strength to his people.
> Praise be to God!
>
> (Psalm 68:35)

One of the biggest challenges in figuring out how God wants to work in our lives is getting our eyes off ourselves. By nature, we are self-centered and self-absorbed. Leadership, however, is by nature other-centered—"whoever wants to become great among you must be your servant," Jesus said (Mark 10:43). Worship gives you something bigger than you and bigger than life to focus on. The more you worship, the more other-centered you become. As a result, God will periodically give you direction in the midst of worship. You may be listening to a song, and the answer to your question comes into focus. You may be singing, and a decision suddenly becomes clear. You may be expressing yourself in prayer, and the next step in your journey reveals itself. This happens because God trusts people who have their eyes off themselves.

I was recently in Israel visiting many of the sites where Jesus carried on his earthly ministry. In Capernaum, Jesus's home base, we learned that this was a strategic city because people would stay there on their way between Damascus and Jerusalem. People from all over would stop here to rest and stock up on supplies. When Jesus performed a miracle, word would spread quickly because travelers would take the news either to Jerusalem or to Damascus.

I took some time there to pray and honor God for the way he launched the gospel, which has become a worldwide movement. As I was doing so, the realization hit me that Jesus had prepared the disciples for exactly what he wanted them to do. Seven of the disciples were from Capernaum, so they had been exposed to the nations of the world all their life. When Jesus instructed them to "make disciples of all nations," they would have had a mental picture of what that meant. Along with this realization was the thought that God has prepared me for what he wants me to do in life. He has been taking steps my whole life to get me ready for his plan.

You can develop habits in your life to get yourself ready to hear from God in worship:

- Attend church regularly so you can participate in a corporate worship experience. Sing during the singing (no matter how you sing), follow the worship leader's instructions, and focus on the words being used to honor God.

- Practice telling God in your personal prayer time how great he is. Review his characteristics and use what is true about him to honor him with your words.

- Play worship music while you go about everyday tasks.

- Ask God to use your times of worship to give you direction in life.

The Word Is Alive

Hebrews 4:12 reveals that "the word of God is alive and active. Sharper than any double-edged sword, it penetrates even to dividing soul and spirit, joints and marrow; it judges the thoughts and attitudes of the heart." Ephesians 6:17 tells us that the word of God is "the sword of the Spirit." This means that the Holy Spirit utilizes the words of the Bible to guide our steps. As you spend time reading and hearing the Bible, you will notice that some verses seem to jump off the page at you. Some of these verses help you feel better about yourself and about life. Others will disturb you and make you aware of some area that God wants to change. As you pay attention to these verses, God leads you toward his plan for you.

It won't happen every day or every week or maybe even every year. But periodically the Bible will come alive in your life. You may be reading it, studying it with friends, listening to it, or meditating on a verse you've committed to memory. You don't have to go looking for it. You simply need to stay consistent in exposing yourself to God's Word. The Spirit of God will use your exposure to the Bible to guide your decisions and commitments to line up with his will. Keep in mind that God wants to lead you more than you want to be led. He will make it obvious so that you don't have to wonder or worry.

When Prayer Just Isn't Enough

Fasting will sharpen your spiritual focus and enable you to gain insight and direction for any decision that is before you. Here are some simple guidelines to follow when you decide to fast.

Set a specific time. The length of your fast is not as important as the fact that you fasted. If you are new to this discipline, start with a short period of time (one meal, half a day, one day). As you get accustomed to this discipline, you can choose to fast for longer periods.

Choose a specific plan for denying yourself food. You can skip all meals for a day. You can skip one meal for seven days in a row. You can skip sugar for forty days and so on. You can skip your favorite TV show in order to spend that time praying. The goal is to deny yourself food (or some other pleasurable activity) to focus on prayer.

Drink lots of water. You do not want to get dehydrated while you are fasting.

If fasting from food, come off your fast gently. Introduce whatever you

denied yourself back into your diet slowly. If you are going to engage
in an intense fast (days without food), consult your physician and the
Campus Crusade for Christ International website devoted to fasting (www.ccci.org/growth/growing-closer-to-god/how-to-fast/index
.aspx). If you have any health concerns at all, always consult your physician first before fasting or changing dietary habits.

Choose a positive attitude. Jesus says in Matthew 6:16-18,

> "When you fast, do not look somber as the hypocrites do,
> for they disfigure their faces to show others they are fasting.
> Truly I tell you, they have received their reward in full. But
> when you fast, put oil on your head and wash your face, so
> that it will not be obvious to others that you are fasting, but
> only to your Father, who is unseen; and your Father, who
> sees what is done in secret, will reward you."

*Spend the time you would normally use preparing and consuming food
to pray.* This is your time to specifically seek God for direction on your
current decision. Jesus also says in Matthew 7:7-8,

> "Ask and it will be given to you; seek and you will find;
> knock and the door will be opened to you. For everyone
> who asks receives; the one who seeks finds; and to the one
> who knocks, the door will be opened."

Accompany your prayer with Bible reading. Jeremiah 36:5-6 sets the
example:

> Then Jeremiah told Baruch, "I am restricted; I cannot go to
> the LORD's temple. So you go to the house of the LORD on
> a day of fasting and read to the people from the scroll the
> words of the LORD that you wrote as I dictated. Read them
> to all the people of Judah who come in from their towns."

Journal your discoveries. As you fast, God will impress verses,
thoughts, and plans on your heart. As you record these insights, they
form together into a decision you can have confidence in.

Mimic the Way the Holy Spirit Thinks

One way to train ourselves to have a cooperative attitude is to mimic the way the Spirit approaches life. We know, of course, that we can never fully do what the Holy Spirit does, but we can focus our thoughts and actions to give him wider access. Mimicking the Spirit is different than trying to be the Spirit. To mimic means we will do what we believe the Spirit would do in the situation we are in with the hope that he will get actively involved in our situation.

This appears to be an intrinsic tendency of mankind. Boys naturally mimic their fathers while daughters mimic their mothers. We also tend to mimic the behaviors of the people we respect. I have noticed all the men in my family use a distinctive expression to communicate "I heard you" or something similar.

"I will be there at 7:00 p.m."

"Gotcha."

"Caleb won his game last weekend. It was fun to watch."

"Gotcha."

"Hey Dad, this Saturday is Eden's birthday party. We would love it if you and Mom can be there."

"Gotcha."

My dad, my brother, all three of my sons, and I use this expression regularly, and none of us ever decided to make it part of our vocabulary. We have simply been mimicking each other for generations so that it is second nature for us.

So, how do we mimic the Spirit?

One way is to choose to think the way the Spirit thinks. The way the Spirit thinks is revealed in the Bible. As you read, hear, and study the Bible, you will become aware of the Spirit's perspective on life and love. You can then choose to adopt the same perspective. The subjects the Holy Spirit focuses on are summarized in Philippians 4:8. "Finally, brothers and sisters, whatever is true, whatever is noble, whatever is right, whatever is pure, whatever is lovely, whatever is admirable—if anything is excellent or praiseworthy—think about such things."

This is a great place to start in mimicking the way the Spirit thinks.

Relieve Spiritual Stress by the Holy Spirit

I don't think I'm telling you anything new when I say that leadership is a battleground. I don't mean to say that there is always conflict in your organization (although it may feel like it to some of you). I am saying, however, that what you are doing is highly significant, so there is a concerted spiritual effort to disrupt your effectiveness. Success in your organization will raise people's confidence, provide for financial needs, help solve problems in people's lives, and draw people together. A well-run organization has so much significant impact that it actually invites conflict.

One of the reasons is spiritual stress. Satan and his cohorts do not want your venture to thrive. He knows your leadership will create stronger people who discover God's plan for their lives and raise strong families. If he can distort your impact on each other, he can distort the progress of the gospel as people become absorbed with interpersonal conflict rather than with the accomplishment of their goals. People may, therefore, grow tense with one another for no particular reason.

You can practice two skills to help minimize the spiritual stress in your leadership environment. The first is to *pray out loud*. When you become aware of tension and conflict, pray first, then talk. Certainly, not all tension and conflict in your relationships are caused by spiritual forces, but they can be one of the causes. Before you venture into solving the problem with your own ingenuity, it is wise to eliminate any possible stress caused by the enemy's lies. Pray a prayer similar to the one below under the heading "Practice the Presence." Often the conflict will evaporate simply because you eliminated the source, which is spiritual rather than relational, by praying out loud. Discernment, of course, is in order as it may not be appropriate to pray out loud among your coworkers; you may want to find a private place.

The other skill you can practice is to *replace lies with truth*. When conflict arises, you can ask, "Is there an obvious lie affecting our interaction?" This is the playground for demons. John 8:44 tells us that Satan is "the father of lies." This is the weapon he uses against believers. He lies to us and tries to convince us the lie is true. When we believe the lie, we create a small opening of influence that demons exploit to get us frustrated with one another. As soon as you identify the lie and pronounce the truth, you disarm the influence causing the conflict.

Often the lies that cause alarms to go off come from our families of origin. Family patterns are strong, and they work hard to repeat themselves generation after generation. Everyone you lead learned these patterns during their most impressionable years, and they bring these patterns to work with them. They are lodged deep within, and they get triggered by emotional responses that inevitably occur.

I was in a meeting with a dedicated group of church leaders when a problem with a staff member came up. This staff member had made a mistake that was having a lingering, negative effect on a significant number of people. It was difficult to discuss since the staff member was the wife of one of the men in the room. We were trying to problem solve together, but it was getting personal for the husband.

I sensed we were tiptoeing around the issue and making little progress, so I emphatically said to the group, "She made a mistake here, and we need to do something or we will lose credibility."

At that, her husband abruptly stood to his feet, threw his church keys on my desk, and angrily said, "She did not make a mistake, and you are making way too big a deal out of this. I don't think I can serve here anymore. I quit." He then stormed out of the room as the rest of us stared at each other in stunned disbelief.

I didn't realize it at the time, but this godly man grew up in an alcoholic home. His dad was unreasonable and would regularly accuse his wife of bad behavior and bad decisions. The few times he tried to stand up for his mom, his dad punished him severely. When he got married, he determined no one would ever treat his wife the way his dad treated his mom. It intensified when they gave birth to a daughter. My statement at the meeting triggered those deep emotions, and he came running to his wife's defense.

I know this about him now because he opened up. After the meeting, I went to his house to see how he was doing and to repair the relationship, if possible. He humbly told me the story about his home and how important it was to be his wife's protector. He did decide not to serve on the board anymore, but his level of self-disclosure cemented trust between us. He continued to be a significant volunteer, and his wife continued to serve on our staff with great effectiveness.

The Spirit of God wants to use these triggers to cause growth in our lives. It is his job to create the growth; it is our job to cooperate. The way we cooperate is through an honest evaluation of the influence of our family of origin. One of the great moments of maturity in our lives is when we ask, "Which traits from my family do I want to keep in my life and which traits do I want to replace with better skills?" When you do this as a leader, you take adult responsibility for your life. When you encourage those you lead to do the same thing, you help them take adult responsibility for their lives. As you can imagine, an organization filled with people taking responsibility will be highly effective.

Practice the Presence

Pray this prayer out loud for five days when you are not in conflict. Then pray this before you begin any tense discussions.

> *Jesus, I thank you for your victory on the cross. I know that your death and resurrection has made me more than a conqueror. Therefore, I humbly stand with you and in your name I command any evil spirits who are around to be quiet and not operate in any way. I announce that I am on your team, and I commit this conversation to you. Please guide the conversation and provide your power to work things out.*

To help you be the best leader you can be, work through the steps below as you evaluate the influence of your family.

Step 1: What is healthy in my family that I want to incorporate into my life?

Step 2: What is unhealthy in my family that I want to replace with more productive behaviors?

Step 3: What productive behavior do I want to practice instead of the unhealthy behavior that gets triggered?

Step 4: Ask the Holy Spirit to give you power to accomplish steps 1 through 3.

Pray Through Scripture

A dynamic interaction exists between the Holy Spirit and the Word of God. The Spirit uses the Word to get our attention, guide our steps, and grow us up. Every step we take, therefore, to apply the Bible to our life in a personal and practical way has a dramatic impact on us. One of the best ways I know to make the Bible personal and practical is to pray through different verses of Scripture. Here are some suggestions for how to effectively pray the Bible over your life:

- Choose verses that apply to your life. The Bible is a very personal book and contains a vast number of promises and instructions. However, some verses are historical in nature and apply to specific circumstances. Caution should be taken in these instances so as not to misapply passages. A good example is Psalm 51:11 where David writes, "Do not take your Holy Spirit from me." In the Old Testament, the Spirit would come upon people for a specific purpose and limited duration. In the New Testament, the Spirit indwells believers and will never be removed from them. This was a very real prayer for David that is no longer necessary in the lives of believers.

- Insert your name or a personal pronoun into the verse where it is appropriate (see the examples of how to do this below).

- Pray these verses over your life out loud.

Examples:

Ephesians 1:17—"I keep asking that the God of our Lord Jesus Christ, the glorious Father, may give [me] the Spirit of wisdom and revelation, so that [I] may know him better."

Colossians 3:9-10,12—"[I] do not lie to [others], since [I] have taken off [my] old self with its practices and have put on the new self, which is being renewed in knowledge in the image of its Creator…[I] clothe [myself] with compassion, kindness, humility, gentleness and patience."

Choose the Opposite

Inside every believer a war is raging. It's the battle between the "old self" and the "new self." The old self is empowered and directed by our natural human nature, which is selfish and deceptive. The new self is empowered and directed by the Holy Spirit, which is other-centered and relationally skillful. In Colossians, Paul lays out the contrast between the old self and the new.

Put to death, therefore, whatever belongs to your earthly nature: sexual immorality, impurity, lust, evil desires and greed, which is idolatry. Because of these, the wrath of God is coming. You used to walk in these ways, in the life you once lived. But now you must also rid yourselves of all such things as these: anger, rage, malice, slander, and filthy language from your lips. Do not lie to each other, since you have taken off your old self with its practices and have put on the new self, which is being renewed in knowledge in the image of its Creator. Here there is no Gentile or Jew, circumcised or uncircumcised, barbarian, Scythian, slave or free, but Christ is all, and is in all.

Therefore, as God's chosen people, holy and dearly loved, clothe yourselves with compassion, kindness, humility, gentleness and patience. Bear with each other and forgive one another if any of you has a grievance against someone. Forgive as the Lord forgave you. And over all these virtues put on love, which binds them all together in perfect unity (Colossians 3:5-14).

As you lead, the Holy Spirit will use the contrast between these two natures to give you guidance. You will notice at times that the people you are leading are operating according to the old self. They may be angry or contentious or fearful or any of a hundred other reactions. As this is happening, the Holy Spirit will prompt you to do the opposite. You will have the sense that you should respond to anger with gentleness, argumentativeness with peace, or timidity with boldness. It will go against your natural inclinations, and you will probably resist it because it makes you feel vulnerable. When you respond in this way, however, you give the Holy Spirit the opportunity to change the hearts and actions of those around you. You have probably noticed that it does not help to point out bad behavior while it is in progress, even when you are right. Instead, it serves only to intensify the behavior you are trying to stop.

Try responding as the Spirit prompts you and see what happens. Colossians 3 refers to this process as "putting off" clothing and "putting on" clothing. The point is that you have a choice, and the choice is usually irritatingly obvious. Negative behavior is like a flashlight that points out the positive behavior the Holy Spirit wants to produce in you.

The following are some habits you can develop to get yourself ready to hear from God as you choose to put on the new self.

- *Practice delaying your response.* When others respond to you in a negative way, count to five before you say or do anything.

- *Practice the opposite behavior.* Ask yourself, "What is the opposite of this negative behavior?" Rather than react to negative words or actions, choose to be positive and encouraging. Then see what God does. A positive result may not happen immediately, but you certainly won't help the situation if you react negatively.

- *Ask God to use your choice of the opposite behavior to improve your organization.*

The most sustainable form of leadership is a reflection of who you are. Jesus announced, "Each tree is recognized by its own fruit...A good man brings good things out of the good stored up in his heart, and an evil man brings evil things out of the evil stored up in his heart. For the mouth speaks what the heart is full of" (Luke 6:44,45-46).

With God's help you can significantly influence others because you will be a leader guided by the Holy Spirit.

Pursue Your Dream

Imagine if leaders didn't lead.

The thought became real to me during the days when Michael Jordan, Larry Bird, and Magic Johnson were dominating the National Basketball Association. I was the president of the youth basketball league in our hometown. I saw a lot of young men and women with dreams in their hearts to become college and professional competitors. We all knew that very few of them would ever make it to that level, but we also knew that what we were doing was important. Without the thousands of youth leagues around the country providing the opportunity for young people to discover their talent, there would not be a big enough player pool to fill the high school teams who would provide talent for the college level and so on. It took every level of involvement, led by ordinary to remarkable leaders, to build a system that could support the professional league.

The incessant need for leaders became even more real to me when I considered my own salvation. I met Jesus in 1976 in an ordinary town in California. In order for me to be exposed to the gospel, the message had to be carried halfway around the world over a course of almost two thousand years. Without the efforts of faithful church leaders and missionaries throughout church history, I would never have known about Jesus and his free gift of eternal life.

Consider the genealogy of Jesus himself in Luke 3. Seventy-five names are listed, and all were necessary in order to bring the Savior into the world. I'm sure you've heard of David, Boaz, Abraham, Isaac, and Jacob, as well as Noah and Adam. I think you would be hard pressed, however, to say anything significant about Serug, Melea, Addi, Jannai, or Heli. We don't know much about them, but they are family leaders who are just as important as the superstars in the lineage of Jesus. You may be a well-known leader or you may be exercising your gifts in an obscure corner of the world. Either way, you are part of the worldwide system that keeps truth on display and organizations productive.

The Rise of Innovation

If leaders didn't lead, the innovations we rely on every day would never have come into existence. We would not have personal computers without the leadership of Bill Gates and Steve Jobs. We would not have appliances that simplify our lives, cars that transport us with ease, or phones that keep us connected.

Preserving Moral Excellence

If leaders didn't lead, the morals of our society would deteriorate at an even more rapid rate than they already are. People naturally tend toward decay, destruction, and disastrous behavior: "For in my inner being I delight in God's law; but I see another law at work in me, waging war against the law of my mind and making me a prisoner of the law of sin at work within me" (Romans 7:22-23).

The evidence of this struggle is rampant. News of sexually transmitted diseases does nothing to slow promiscuity. Reports of overdoses, fatal car crashes, and disease are ineffective in curbing people's appetite for abusing drugs and alcohol. Bob Goldman asked 198 world-class athletes if they would take a magic drug that would guarantee victory in any competition but would kill them five years after they took it. More than half of those athletes said yes![1]

On the relationship front, it has been established that couples who forego premarital training or who cohabitate before marriage have a higher risk of divorce, and yet, according to the National Institute of Child Health and Human Development, more than half of all marriages in the US now begin with cohabitation. [2] These truths can be disheartening except that leaders see the needs and are stirred in their hearts to do something about it, such as Bob Moorehead who comments:

- We spend more, but have less, we buy more, but enjoy less.

- We have bigger houses and smaller families, more conveniences, but less time.

- We have more degrees, but less sense, more knowledge, but less judgment, more experts, but more problems, more medicine, but less wellness.

- We drink too much, smoke too much, spend too recklessly, laugh too little, drive too fast, get too angry too quickly, stay up too late, get up too tired, pray too seldom, and watch too much TV…

- We've learned how to make a living, but not a life, we've added years to life, not life to years…

- We've learned to rush, but not wait, we have higher incomes, but lower morals, more food, but less appeasement, more acquaintances, but fewer friends, more effort, but less success…

- These are the days of two incomes, but more divorce, of fancier houses, but broken homes.

- These are the days of quick trips, disposable diapers, throwaway morality, one night stands, overweight bodies, and pills that do everything from cheer, to quiet, to kill…

- Today, many want to gain the world at the "mere" expense of their souls.

- Evil is contemplated and performed with both

hands, yet we cannot lift a finger for our fellow
man.

May God have mercy on our souls. Pray without ceasing.
Let each of us examine our own ways. [3]

If leaders don't comment on these developments and call the rest of
us to action, no one will. Only leaders have the courage, passion, and
boldness to point out what is morally wrong in our society and offer
solutions that protect the hearts of people.

Guardians of Organization

If leaders didn't lead, disorganization would be the norm. I am
amazed how much leadership energy it takes to keep people on track
with their eye on the prize. The apostle Paul said, "I do not run like
someone running aimlessly; I do not fight like a boxer beating the air.
No, I strike a blow to my body and make it my slave so that after I
have preached to others, I myself will not be disqualified for the prize"
(1 Corinthians 9:26-27). That attitude is rare and must be fostered by
those in charge.

For instance, during my fifteen years as a lead pastor, I had to
develop two habits to keep our worship team focused and running
on fresh energy. When it was time to start our first service, I had to
say to our worship leader, "It's time to start." Over time, I assumed the
team would become more intent on starting on time, but they would
regularly get caught up talking with one another about the impact of
the service. They committed to the inspirational side of leading while
remaining casual about the management of time.

Then, when it was time to start the second service, I would remind
everyone involved, "Keep up first-service energy in the second service."
The tendency was for people to let down after the first "performance"
and rob those who were coming later of their best efforts. We did grow
to the point where I didn't have to be the one to prompt the team, but
the need for someone to do the prompting never went away.

This is the nature of sheep. Jesus said, "I am the good shepherd; I
know my sheep and my sheep know me" (John 10:11). Sheep need

direction, reminders, and constant oversight. They need to be protected and provided for. One of the saddest things Jesus said during his earthly ministry had to do with the lack of leadership among his people: "When he saw the crowds, he had compassion on them, because they were harassed and helpless, like sheep without a shepherd" (Matthew 9:36). Without the watchful eye of the shepherd, they wander, starve, and grow vulnerable to attacks. By declaring that we are sheep, Jesus delivered an ongoing mandate for leaders.

When I took over leadership for a small-group ministry at a Southern California church, I was fascinated how a little organizational leadership ignited a new level of enthusiasm. We decided to set up a structure that would harness the abilities of what we referred to as B-level leaders. A-level leaders took initiative with just an idea. All we needed to do with these leaders was make a suggestion and they would run with it. B-level leaders would implement whatever program we set up. They found security in lesson plans that were laid out for them, announcements that were printed for them, weekly training on CDs to prepare them for their meeting, and the ability to pick up on Sunday all printed materials needed for their group that week. The motivation to be involved in small groups was already there. The willingness to commit to a weekly gathering to learn together and support one another already existed. The one thing lacking was the leadership plan to harness the energy. Once we provided the organizational plan, small-group attendance doubled in a short period of time.

Dealing with Distractions

If leaders didn't lead, people would become distracted and aimless. The book of Judges is a vivid reminder of what happens when leaders don't lead. When Joshua was guiding the nation, things were good. "The people served the LORD throughout the lifetime of Joshua and of the elders who outlived him and who had seen all the great things the LORD had done for Israel" (Judges 2:7). After his death, "another generation grew up who knew neither the LORD nor what he had done for Israel" (2:10). In the leaderless vacuum, "the Israelites did evil in the eyes of the LORD and served the Baals. They forsook the LORD...

[and] followed and worshiped various gods of the peoples around them. They aroused the LORD's anger" (2:11-12).

I become acutely aware of the need for quality, committed leaders whenever I take inventory of developments in our society. An irrational morality is arising that sounds intelligent, compassionate, and modern when in reality it is immorality in new clothes. What used to be recognized as immorality is now referred to as alternative lifestyles. Strong moral convictions are now labeled bigoted and hateful. The taking of a human life has been reduced to a health-care issue. Religious liberty is being sacrificed on the altar of political pressure.

This type of morality appeals to the pride in the human heart because we mistakenly think we can make up the rules without consequences. We pay lip service to the detrimental effects, but we are unwilling to give up our pride for real solutions. The only hope for change is in leaders rising up who will call us to accountability and inspire us to pursue spiritual, ethical, moral, and relational excellence. In the absence of real leaders, people will reduce their behavior to various levels of mediocrity.

It Will Take Time

Without a doubt, the most important project of Solomon's life was building the temple. It was the rallying point for the nation of Israel. It was the daily reminder of the power, majesty, and authority of God Almighty. People would see the sun shine off the golden structure and remember that God was in their midst.

Getting it to that point, however, took time and a lot of work: "The foundation of the temple of the LORD was laid in the fourth year…In the eleventh year…the temple was finished in all its details according to its specifications. He had spent seven years building it" (1 Kings 6:37-38).

The project was described in one chapter, but it took seven years to build. The process required strategic planning, preparation of the building materials, attention to details, countless hours of both skilled and unskilled labor, and consistent reminders of the purpose for this project. It was a magnificent structure that was made possible only with perseverance and perspiration.

It is all the more intriguing when you consider 1 Corinthians 6:19, "Do you not know that your bodies are temples of the Holy Spirit, who is in you, whom you have received from God?" In the days of Solomon, God "dwelt" in the temple built by human hands. Today, God "dwells" in us. We are the temple. We are the consistent reminder that God is powerful, loving, and living among us. The implications deserve our daily attention:

- Our lives are worthwhile projects.

- It will take time, so we need to stay at it.

- We will grow best if we have a strategic plan.

- We need to pay attention to the significant details of our lives as effectiveness usually comes down to the little things.

- Reminders of our purpose are helpful.

- We need the help of others to complete our development.

- We need to highly value the preparation phases because important projects take time!

Like most of us, I am generally in a hurry to be what it will take time to become. I want to be smarter now, stronger now, and more successful now even though I know that some things just take time.

I flew from Boston to Orange County, California, last winter. On paper it was an eight-hour journey, including a stopover in Dallas. The weather had other plans, however, so we spent a couple of hours circling the Dallas airport. Running low on fuel, we had to divert to Tulsa, Oklahoma, to fill the tanks before returning to Dallas, only to circle for another hour. I knew we had been at it longer than any of us planned when the flight attendant looked at his watch and said, "Wow, we could have been in London by now!"

Of course, my connecting flight to California was cancelled, and the next flight with available seats didn't leave until late in the evening.

When I arrived at my front door at midnight, I realized my eight-hour journey had been transformed into a twenty-one-hour excursion of character development. It was a vivid reminder that some things just take time!

You are an important project, and your development as a leader will take time. The world with all its complexity, web of relationships, and challenges needs your leadership today. It will need your leadership tomorrow and seven years from now. As long as God gives you breath, your skills and influence will be needed to help others grow and organizations function.

As you lead, keep in mind the words Moses spoke to Joshua, "Be strong and courageous...The LORD himself goes before you and will be with you; he will never leave you nor forsake you. Do not be afraid; do not be discouraged" (Deuteronomy 31:7-8).

As you courageously pursue your dream, may God do through you what is beyond you!

Introduction: Leadership Is You

1. *The Visitor*, April 1984, www.sermonillustrations.com/a-z/p/problem_solving.htm.

2. Adapted from "Don't Quit—The ultimate goal of taking the hill…," www.leadership-skills -for-life.com/dont-quit.html.

3. "Abraham Lincoln: Leadership Case Study," *Leadership with You*, www.leadership-with-you .com/abraham-lincoln-leadership.html.

4. "Gandhi, Mohandas Karamchand (1869–1948)," *Martin Luther King, Jr. and the Global Freedom Struggle*, http://mlk-kpp01.stanford.edu/index.php/encyclopedia/encyclopedia/ enc_gandhi_mohandas_karamchand_1869_1948/.

5. "Abraham Lincoln," www.leadership-with-you.com/abraham-lincoln-leadership.html.

6. "The Balloon Story," www.businessballs.com/stories.htm#stories.

Chapter 1: Decide to Be a Leader

1. Since the chromosome pairing for males is XY and for females it's XX.

2. Henning Mankell, "The Art of Listening," *New York Times*, December 20, 2011, www.nytimes .com/2011/12/11/opinion/sunday/in-africa-the-art-of-listening.html.

Chapter 2: Decide to Pursue Your Personal Vision

1. "Sample Vision Statements," www.skills2lead.com/sample-vision-statements.html.

2. Mike Wynn and Joseph Lord, "Kentucky Fans Riot after Defeat of Louisville in Final Four," *Courier-Journal*, 1 April 2012, http://content.usatoday.com/communities/campusrivalry/ post/2012/04/kentucky-fans-riot-violence-fires-louisville-win/1#.T3oVP9XleSp.

Chapter 3: Decide to Be Ready

1. "Powerful Kid Magic," *Only Funny Stories*, www.onlyfunnystories.com/Powerful-Kids-Magic -stories.asp.

Chapter 4: Decide to Be Real

1. "The Priest and the Politician Story," www.businessballs.com/stories.htm#stories.

Chapter 5: Decide to Team Up

1. "A Touching Story," http://gatewaytojesus.com/inspirationalstoriespage1.html.

2. "The Blind Men and the Road Story," www.businessballs.com/stories.htm#stories.

Chapter 7: Decide to Be Relational

1. Rick Noland, "Van Epp Is Making Strides," *Medina-Gazette*, 21 September 2007, http://medinagazette.northcoastnow.com/2007/09/21/van-epp-is-making-strides/.

2. Daniel J. Canary, Tara M. Emmers-Sommer with Sandra Faulkner, *Sex and Gender Differences in Personal Relationships* (New York: The Guilford Press, 1997), 98.

Chapter 8: Decide to Identify the Influencers

1. You can see the play at time code 1:30 of *Larry Csonka Highlights*, www.youtube.com/watch?v=sXLEE_5IODw.

2. "Logic 101," http://gatewaytojesus.com/inspirationalstoriespage2.html.

3. Diane, "Story of Influence II," http://get2clear.com/2009/03/18/story-of-influence-ii/.

Chapter 9: Decide to Rally to Risk

1. "The Mechanic and the Surgeon Story," www.businessballs.com/stories.htm#stories.

2. Katy Finneran, "The Greatest Risks They Ever Took," *Forbes*, 21 January 2010, www.forbes.com/2010/01/20/gucci-indy500-letterman-entreprenuer-management-risk-greatest_slide_12.html.

3. These principles are developed more fully in our book *Men Are Like Waffles—Women Are Like Spaghetti* (Eugene, OR: Harvest House Publishers, 2001).

4. Finneran, "Greatest Risks," www.forbes.com/2010/01/20/gucci-indy500-letterman-entreprenuer-management-risk-greatest_slide_35.html.

Chapter 10: Decide to Seek Supernatural Support

1. For more information about this organization see www.cru.org.

Conclusion: Pursue Your Dream

1. Steven M. Horwitz, "Anabolic Steroids: The Road to the Gold or the Road to the Grave," Capital Sports Injury Center, www.marylandsportsinjurycenter.com/ster.html.

2. Sheri and Bob Stritof, "Cohabitation Facts and Statistics," http://marriage.about.com/od/cohabitation/qt/cohabfacts.htm.

3. Bob Moorehead, "The Paradox of Our Age," http://gatewaytojesus.com/inspirationalstoriespage2.html.

Bill Farrel and his wife, Pam, are relationship specialists who help people discover how to be "Love Wise." They are international speakers and authors of over thirty-five books, including the best-selling *Men Are Like Waffles—Women Are Like Spaghetti* (over 300,000 sold). A few of their other books include *Red-Hot Monogamy*; *The 10 Best Decisions a Man Can Make*; and *The 10 Best Decisions a Parent Can Make*.

Bill and Pam are frequent guests on radio and television, and their writing has appeared in numerous magazines and newspapers. Bill has experience as a senior pastor, youth pastor, and pastor to small groups. Pam has experience as a director of women, pastor's wife, and mentor. Their books have been translated into over sixteen languages. They have been happily married for over thirty years and are parents to three children, a daughter-in-law, two granddaughters, and one grandson. The Farrels live in San Diego, California.

To contact the Farrels or learn more about their other resources:
www.Love-Wise.com
Love-Wise
3755 Avocado Boulevard, #414
La Mesa, CA 91941
(800) 810-4449
info@Love-Wise.com
Like Bill and Pam Farrel on Facebook
Follow Bill Farrel or Pam Farrel on Twitter

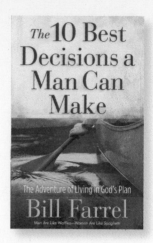

The 10 Best Decisions a Man Can Make
The Adventure of Living in God's Plan

Men today have important decisions to make about family, career, and ministry. Sometimes the choices can seem overwhelming, and men end up making decisions by default—by doing what comes naturally rather than by carefully thought-out principles. In *The 10 Best Decisions a Man Can Make*, popular author and speaker Bill Farrel gives men the hands-on decision-making tools they need to make the kinds of choices they won't regret. Farrel encourages men to discover the joy of finding their place in God's plan as they

- explore the positive benefits of making healthy decisions
- discover their personal pace in life and make decisions in keeping with that pace
- develop a plan for godliness that relieves the burden of self-effort
- learn to make decisions based on personal character rather than what feels right at the moment

The 10 Best Decisions a Man Can Make will empower men to pursue God's best and to achieve true success in the adventure of their lives.

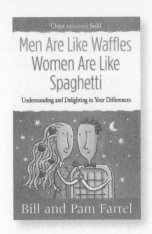

Men Are Like Waffles—Women Are Like Spaghetti
Understanding and Delighting in Your Differences

Over 300,000 sold!

Bill and Pam Farrel offer biblical wisdom, solid insight, and humorous anecdotes—all served up in just the right combination so that readers can feast on enticing ways to

- keep communication cooking
- let gender differences work for—not against—them
- help each other relieve stress
- achieve fulfillment in romantic relationships
- coordinate parenting so kids get the best of both Mom and Dad

The Farrels explain why a man is like a waffle (each element of his life is in a separate box) and a woman is like spaghetti (everything in her life touches everything else). End-of-chapter questions and exercises make this unique and fun look at the different ways men and women regard life a terrific tool not only for marriage but also for a reader's relationships at work, at home, at church, and with friends.

Men Are Like Waffles—Women Are Like Spaghetti Devotional Study Guide

Ideal for individual or group study, small group leaders will find this guide a useful tool for leading couples in biblically based discussions, and couples who choose to go through it together will find the guide perfect for a create-your-own marriage retreat.

A Couple's Journey with God

Bill and Pam Farrel, authors of the bestselling *Men Are Like Waffles—Women Are Like Spaghetti*, bring their keen insights into relationships to these devotions that celebrate marriage, encourage open communication, and provide meaningful ways for husbands and wives to draw closer together.

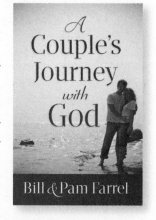

Our busy world often pulls couples apart, but it doesn't have to be that way. Spending time together each day in devotion and prayer will strengthen and bring joy to a relationship as couples learn to connect their love with God's wisdom.

A Couple's Journey with God will expose readers to practical ideas for staying in love, personal tips for great interactions, and passionate prompts for adding that extra spark to their relationship. It's the perfect book for all couples at any stage of life and relationship.

To learn more about Harvest House books and
to read sample chapters, log on to our website:

www.harvesthousepublishers.com

HARVEST HOUSE PUBLISHERS
EUGENE, OREGON